11-18-74

ADMISSIONS

ADMISSIONS
Notes from a
Woman Psychiatrist

by

JUDITH BENETAR, M.D.

Charterhouse

NEW YORK

To Dublin

ADMISSIONS

Copyright © 1974 by Judith Benetar, M. D.

All rights reserved, including the right to reproduce
this book, or parts thereof, in any form, except for
the inclusion of brief quotations in a review.

Library of Congress Catalog Card Number: 74–82447

ISBN 0–88327–041–2

MANUFACTURED IN THE UNITED STATES OF AMERICA

1825592

Part One

"Shit, I'm late," I say and get on the bus. From the window, Central Park looks still and graceful in the early-morning light. A few leaves spiral softly to the earth.

"Lady, you forgot to pay. Whaddaya think this is, anyway?" The driver mumbles under his breath about my sanity, and I consider with some amusement that I am supposed to be the expert on his. In silence, I take a seat under an ad for Wrigley's Spearmint Gum. Two black schoolgirls chatter in the seat in front of me. Their giggles and intimacy underline my sense of isolation, and I feel a wave of resentment that I am on call for the next twenty-four hours, insulated from other people in a way perhaps only doctors come to know and understand.

The tension, the vigilance, the concern and worry, the special strain of psychiatric emergency call is hard to define, but it requires something from me that I seldom had to exercise when I was an intern in medicine and surgery. There is a something more subtle and strenuous about this psychiatric stuff. Two whole people face to face maybe.

"The cardiac arrest" or "the GI bleeder" or the "Could you come up and draw a blood sugar, doctor?" of my internship left me physically fatigued after a night on call, but otherwise reasonably intact, because when the existential pain or absurdity threatened to rear its ugly head, I could escape into people as pieces or electrolyte abnormalities. "Doctor, the gall bladder on F-4 has spiked a temp. . . ."

But this work, though it has its own hiding places and

cop-outs, usually manages to find me and repeatedly confront me with aspects of myself, my innate humanity or lack of it. And twenty-four hours without respite gets to me in ways I find hard to define. Attempts to hear, see, and maybe sometimes even begin to comprehend and tentatively reach out to people in emotional trouble. I find myself thinking of grade school somehow: Look both ways, Listen, and Cross Carefully when the coast is clear. Except that in school they don't tell you about times when the coast is never clear and there are no green lights to help.

The bus rumbles to a halt, and the two little girls get off, still chattering. The doors close and someone coughs. There is a moment of overwhelming loneliness, which passes. A man behind me wonders aloud to his companion why so many buses smell like bug spray. Indeed the bus is reeking. His friend responds with a non sequitur about the football score, and the conversation goes on, neither hearing the other, both somehow animated and curiously satisfied with their lack of verbal communication.

The next stop is mine. I glance by habit at the incongruous one-story structure on the corner with its green copper dunce-cap roof surrounded and overwhelmed by the later buildings. A plaque above its door announces that the Dr. William Stevens Operating Theatre was built in 1861. Microscopes and test tubes in the windows now. Neat people in white coats. Barely a memory of buckets and bodies and endless arguments about antisepsis.

The revolving door of the Castle Building squeaks in the cold and damp. The porter, or whatever he calls himself, is all smiles.

"One of the elevators is stuck again today, doc. You'll have to wait awhile, I'm afraid. The other one's on Castle ten." He pushes both black buttons and bangs importantly on the door.

WHAT IS THIS MAN DOING, PUSHING BUTTONS ALL DAY? I start to ask myself, but stop, avoiding the futility and pain, the myth of Sisyphus déjà vu.

"Yeah, here it comes now, doc. Have a good day."

"You too, Ralph."

I take the elevator to Castle 12, the third of four psychiatric floors in the hospital. Elaine is waiting, staring at the wall, unmoving.

Clara, a heavy-set, jolly psychiatric nurse dressed in blue slacks and blue polka-dot blouse, sees me and comes out of the nurses' station.

"Judy, Elaine's been here since six this morning. She said she had an appointment with you, but wouldn't tell me what time. Then she sat down there and started grooving on the wall. I haven't been able to get a word out of her since."

"Thanks for trying, Clara."

Above Elaine's chair is a painting of the ocean in a storm. Across the hall, directly in her line of vision, a blank wall. Today she has abandoned her usual costume of patched jeans and gray "Blessington High" sweatshirt for a white peasant blouse and ill-fitting brown skirt, white socks, and thready, ancient sneakers. The clownlike effect fails at her face. For the thousandth time, I wonder how someone who spends half her time in a special hell and the rest on a tenuous tightrope can manage to retain an exquisite and unsullied beauty. At twenty-five, she is a veteran of fifteen years of journeys to and from various state hospitals, emotional and physical assaults by her family, and at least two hideous suicide attempts.

Her most self-abasing gesture had been to swallow a bottle of tranquilizers and crawl into a sewer to die. It failed when the stench made her vomit. She sat there another couple of hours waiting to die before she realized that the medication hadn't been absorbed, then dragged herself home and slept in her filthy clothes for the rest of the day.

Elaine's life outside hospitals had been a marginal existence in self-selected hovels in the worst parts of the city, with occasional attempts at outpatient psychotherapy. We had been working together for about ten months, since the end of my first year of psychiatric residency.

I look at the lovely head and wonder at the ironic contrast of the psychotic nightmare inside. Helen of Troy in some continual, grotesque Halloween celebration.

"Hi."

A flicker of long, dark lashes. The face remains impassive, a piece of sculpture, vacant eyes contemplating a void.

"C'mon, Elaine. Not again. Not now. It's been ages since you did this last. We have a lot to talk about, and this wastes so much of your time. Don't go there again. C'mon . . . Elaine." My hand on her shoulder and the eyes come to life. Her head turns toward me and she looks up in a confusion I always have to tell myself is probably genuine. "Ah! She lives! Hi."

"Hi, Judy—Dr. Benetar—Judy. I—what time is it?"

"It's quarter past nine. Between my lateness and your statue routine, we're doing a beautiful job of screwing up your hour. C'mon, let's go up."

She takes my hand and stands like a four-year-old child, one sock falling below her ankle.

"I'm sorry, Judy. I couldn't help it."

"Well, I *could* help being late. I'm sorry, too. C'mon, let's go upstairs."

She gathers up her belongings with her free hand—a brightly colored cloth shoulder bag someone brought her from Greece; the loose-leaf notebook that is her constant companion; a Macy's shopping bag of odds and ends, which I know includes a piece of apple-tree branch broken accidentally in the spring when Elaine was trying to retrieve a kitten; and a primer of English grammar. When she was about eight, a teacher had mistaken her torment and unresponsiveness for stupidity and deafness and advised her family to put her in a school for retarded and disabled children. In the beginning, she had mocked and beaten some of her more handicapped classmates, but then felt sorry for them when they cried. A few months later, she was helping the teacher take care of them and had learned the language of the deaf and dumb fluently. It became one of the happier experiences of her life, but she was discharged when her instructors eventually realized she was different from the others. In all, she was at the school for just over two years. There was, in fact, nothing wrong with Elaine's ears, and her IQ, recently tested, was over 130.

Clara watches us start up the stairway to the interns' and residents' office.

"Feeling better, Elaine?"

"Yes, thanks, Clara. Clara, you didn't tell her, did you?"

Clara waves noncommittally and turns to the medication cart, shouting ludicrously over her shoulder, "Pills, people! Come and get 'um while they're hot. Medication! Med-i-kay-*shun!*"

We turn the corner before any of the sixteen current inpatients on the floor come sifting sleepily out of their rooms or from breakfast in the day room.

"Tell me what, Elaine? Secrets?"

"No. No secrets, Judy. I just asked her not to tell you what time I got here. Did she?"

"Yes, she did. What's that all about?"

We reach the office and, as usual, I fumble clumsily for the right set of keys somewhere at the bottom of a hopelessly chaotic handbag. Elaine is shifting uneasily from one foot to the other.

"Um—it isn't about anything. I just couldn't sleep, so I came in early."

"Ah! At last!" I hold up the keys triumphantly and open the door with a flourish. A half-smile from Elaine.

"And besides, it was cold in my apartment, Judy. . . . *Really!*"

"Okay, Elaine."

She sits on the edge of a chair. The room is stifling. I excuse myself and open a cleverly designed window with many tiny white-framed panes. The window opens outward to an angle of about thirty degrees, allowing some six inches of ventilation. The effect is decorative, but the intent, of course, is that it be jump-proof. For financial reasons, I suppose, only the inpatient building is supplied with these special windows. In the past year, the outpatient building across the street has lost two psychiatric patients through its standard window frames.

"Elaine, I just have to call the operator and let her know where I am. I'm on call for the emergency room today."

She nods and starts to slip into another frozen universe.

"Elaine, don't go back there again! Cut it out, now!" I say rather sharply. She shudders. While I am on the phone with the operator, her mood abruptly changes, and she sits back in the chair, crossing her legs Indian fashion. Her deep-set blue eyes begin to study me intently. There are times I think she can read my backbone.

When I hang up, Elaine says, "Oh!" and dives into the shopping bag excitedly. She finds a square package hastily wrapped in newspaper, tears off the crumpled pages, and hands me a flat cardboard box.

"What's this?"

"It's for you. Open it. But be careful. . . ."

Fragile as butterfly wings, tiny blue flowers with translucent tendril stems had been delicately, invisibly pasted on a piece of coarse green paper from the Kiddy Cut-Out Set she had bought last month. There was an almost Oriental care and beauty about it. I wondered aloud about the hours of patience and concentration it must have taken her.

"Elaine, this is a rare gift. It's incredibly beautiful."

"Do you really like it? I picked the flowers last summer and pressed them in a dictionary I have at home."

"It's lovely. Thank you." It would be one of the treasures

of my life. Her prolonged silence makes me look up.

"Judy, do you hate me?"

"It's been a long time since you asked me that. Maybe you'd like to let me in on what's happening today?"

"Yes, okay, I'll try, but first, do you?"

"Would I spend three hours a week for ten months so far, rain or shine, wind or snow, heat wave or blizzard, voluntarily yet, with someone I hate? Me? A brilliant, budding psychiatrist who's supposed to know something about the choices she makes in life?"

"Um—no, I guess not. I guess even I wouldn't do a thing like that."

"Well, hallelujah, then maybe we're getting somewhere!"

We both laugh and some of the tension recedes. The next silence is a working one. Maybe the most difficult problem during my residency has been to differentiate qualities of silence. Including, and most difficult, my own.

"Treek started laughing at me Wednesday night after I saw you. He hasn't bothered me for weeks, Judy."

"And what did the old sage have to say for himself?"

Treek had first started visiting Elaine when she was seven. Her mother had sent her to the cellar as punishment for making too much noise, and he had come to console her. Until adolescence, he had been a constant and warm companion, reassuring her, whispering in her ear when her stepfather bound her hands and whipped her in the garage, urging her to laugh at the darkness and cobwebs in the cellar. At that time, too, she could make him come and go at will. Then, during puberty, he began to grow sullen, and it was no longer easy to get him to leave.

Eventually, Treek became a malevolent tyrant, able even to manipulate the environment. There were times he could make the walls weep and scream, but mostly he amused himself by laughing and shouting obscenities at Elaine. Once, during her late teens, he had left her alone for a period of several months when she was in therapy with a woman doctor at a state hospital. The doctor moved to another institution, and Treek returned full force, venomous and unrelenting. About a week later, Elaine made her first suicide attempt. She snatched a letter opener from her new doctor's desk and drove it into her abdomen. Exploratory surgery revealed remarkably little damage, and she was fully ambulatory in a few days. Before the operation and during the immediate post-op period, Treek had giggled and murmured saccharine sarcasms: "Poor dear, does her 'ittle tummy hurt? Oh, what terrible pain she must be in. . . . My, My. Don't worry, sweetie, if you behave yourself, maybe you can avoid gangrene and crotch rot. Hee, hee . . . But maybe. . . ."

As she began to recuperate, he had grown more openly hostile and vicious. "Stupid whore! You can't even kill yourself properly. Now the world's stuck with you again, scum bag. You really fuck things up, don't you. Bitch!" The tirade lasted for weeks. Since then, Treek had waxed or waned, depending on circumstance, environment, and Elaine's degree of vulnerability. In the ten months of treatment with me, he had been an intermittent problem with which, as a neophyte resident, I mostly had to deal creatively. By trial and error, I had found it useful at different times either to embark with Elaine on an allegorical journey, or to ignore her references to Treek entirely and deal with recent interactions between her and me that may have somehow related to his sudden appearances on the scene.

Elaine shifted in her chair. "He laughed and said you were reaching your toleration point, like everyone else in my life. I tried to argue with him and said, 'No, you're wrong, Treek. Not the greatest Panda of them all!' [beings outside the world of Elaine and Treek were all Pandas], but he just laughed again."

"Oh. And this happened after we met on Wednesday and has been going on ever since?"

"Yes, more or less."

"Wow, must have been some heavy stuff going on here Wednesday between you and me. Got any ideas, Elaine?"

Silence. An anxious one, but a silence I choose not to interrupt. I watch a tugboat on the river. It has begun to rain again.

"You wouldn't let me sit on the floor anymore!" she finally blurts out. "When we started in January, you said I could do anything I wanted in these sessions except break things and be physically violent, and now you won't let me anymore! Doesn't that mean you're getting fed up with me and want me to act like a Panda or else get out?"

She stops abruptly, surprised at her outburst and suddenly afraid of my response. She reaches for my hand in quiet desperation.

"Gee, Elaine, I don't remember telling you not to sit on the floor anymore. I told you how it makes me feel when you sit on the floor—"

"Isn't that the same thing?"

"No, I think those are different things. One is a command; the other is a statement of how I feel, which you may *interpret* as a command, but in fact to which you may choose to respond in any one of a number of ways. . . . Do you remember how I said it makes me feel?"

"I think so. . . . You said it makes you feel very big and powerful and that I seem little and weak, like a child."

"Yes, and I think I mentioned that it makes me uncomfortable that we should be so unequal, not only in your head, but also when you're physically seated so much lower than I am. When we started, it was a bit different, because you were out of it so much of the time. But we've come a long way together, and it has a different feeling now. By the way, how does it feel sitting in a chair today?"

"Different—strange. Not like me. Not like I really am. I feel like I don't belong here—scary. But it's interesting in a funny kind of way. . . ." Embarrassed, thoughtful, she picks a piece of lint from her skirt.

"And what do you think would happen if you sat on the floor today?"

Her eyes widen. "Boy, then you'd really reach your toleration point. You'd really hate me then. You'd probably never want to see me again."

"C'mon, Elaine, you're making me into a tyrant. Is that what you really expect would happen?"

She looks genuinely puzzled. "I don't know, Judy. I don't know what would happen."

"Well, how could you find out?"

"How could I find out?"

"Yes. What could you do to find out what would happen?"

A look of bewilderment, followed by sudden realization, and then an unexpected, barely concealed glee.

"Sit on the floor!" she almost shouts. After a moment of frightened hesitation, Elaine is on the floor in a flash, cross-legged again, delighted.

"How do you feel now?"

"Great!"

A subtle, instantaneous change in her face has appeared with her descent to the floor, and she asks in a tiny, singsong voice, "Judy, why is it so hard to spell English?"

I ask her if she notices any difference.

"Yes. I feel like a little kid asking her mother why the sky is blue." As an afterthought, she adds defiantly, "Okay, so what?"

"So, how does it make you feel, knowing that I'm uncomfortable with that kind of relationship with you now?"

After a long, serious pause, she says quietly with profound honesty, "It makes me feel good. I'm in control." Her insight staggers both of us and catches me completely off guard. She has recognized the paradox of the infant— that in its helplessness lies its power. Intelligence and courage like this may decide a direction and an outcome for Elaine. But I temper my enthusiasm and remind myself that these same elements can and have been used as vicious instruments of self-mortification.

She stands up and looks at me. "You're wonderful," she says. "Magic."

Oh, god. From the sublime to the absurd. Here we go again with "the greatest Panda" business, the attempt to undo what she has just accomplished.

"Elaine. Stop and think very, very carefully. Who just figured all that out? Who?"

With great embarrassment, she manages, "I did, I guess. We did together. But you—"

"No more. Let's stop right there for today. I couldn't take another ounce of this magic shit. Okay?"

"Okay . . ."

She starts to gather her things.

"Judy, could I ask you one more thing, not about the magic or anything like that? . . . What's the difference between being sick and well?"

"Well, for you that magic stuff is part of it—thinking you're worthless and everyone else is godlike. But that's a big question, Elaine. I don't know if I know enough even to make a stab at a reasonable answer."

"But just off the top of your head, what would you say?"

Her eyes search mine, and I feel her reading my backbone again.

"I don't know, Elaine," I try feebly, "I guess it's more painful to be sick."

"You mean there's pain when you're well, too?"

"Yeah, a lot of the time. But I suppose not to the degree that you experience it. It doesn't usually take complete control the way it seems to sometimes with you. I guess that may be part of the answer. Even if it's partly an illusion, people who are well have some sense of control over their pain, their feelings; whereas yours seem to have control of you most of the time. But I'm sure it's more complicated than that, and I'm a lousy philosopher. . . . You've obviously been thinking about the whole thing, Elaine; what do you think about it?"

"Well, I guess control might have something to do with it. But I was trying to sort it out in terms of you and me, Judy. And even though you're more disciplined and busier than I am, you seem to be freer somehow. I remembered something Agnes de Mille once said about ballet. It was about how after years of training and discipline and practice, there comes a day when all of a sudden you're not aware of your feet anymore. And it's like flying. . . ."

There is something wondrous and unfathomable and vaguely laughable about us human creatures. An hour ago, this lucid, poetic woman was staring at a wall. What in god's name happened between us in that hour? How does one measure the impact of human beings on each other? The whole thing baffles me, and I guess it's not supposed to. I keep hoping my bewilderment has to do with my inexperience, that one day with study and supervision and several hundred scholarly books, it will all become clear. But I wonder— Einstein said,

> If I have learned one thing in pondering throughout a long life, it is this, that we are much further from a deeper insight into the elementary processes than most of our contemporaries believe . . . so that noisy celebrations are definitely not very appropriate to the actual state of affairs.

"Beat it, woman. I have work to do."
"Have a good day, Judy. Hope the e.r. isn't too bad."
"Yeah, me too. . . ."

She and the shopping bag disappear down the stairs. I close the door and stare out the window, wanting not to think or feel for a moment. The tugboat is gone, and in the heavy mist, the edges of the river are hard to define. Twelve stories below, the streets are slick and wet. Traffic is mov-

ing slowly and some of the cars have turned on their lights.
At the crossings, darkly dressed people huddled under
darker umbrellas waiting for the light to change. And the
association to Ireland and John is unavoidable. . . .

*Meeting furtively on back streets of Dublin, or in Phoenix Park
with its cows and tiny deer grazing somewhere near our parking
place. A man's setter ran toward us through the luminous grass,
his golden-red feathers flowing out behind him, all grace and radi-
ance. Rarely, when we had a luxury of time, we wandered the cliff
walks of Howth, the waves smashing furiously a thousand feet
below, great gray gulls screaming in the wind around us. Shivering
in the constant damp, we would steam up the windows of his car
with our passion and anxiety and finally abandon caution and
control and find some ingenious position to make love on those
ridiculous seats. Afterward, he would wrap me warmly, protectively, in his coat, stroke my hair, and apologize for the accommo-
dations. . . . In the beginning, we were really incredibly reckless.
When I consider now what we risked that day on the table of the
Board of Directors half an hour before his meeting. Impossible
paradox of a man who wrote and taught poetry and administrated
an advisory board almost as an afterthought.*

*Our improbable relationship had begun in my final year of
medical school. At a pub called The Strawberry Beds, a boy of
maybe twelve had set down my chicken-sandwich-and-glass-of-
stout lunch.*

*"Will there be anything else, miss?" he'd asked in a hoarse voice
that was struggling with puberty.*

*I'd shaken my head absentmindedly, then looked up to see him
still standing there in front of the table holding his serving tray,
waiter's towel draped over his right arm.*

"Yes?"

*"If there's nothin' more, that will be five shillings sixpence
please, miss."*

I'd paid him, and with a slight bow, he'd said, "Thanks very much, and enjoy your lunch, miss," and returned to the kitchen.

I'd begun on my sandwich and resumed preoccupations about my troubled marriage. Our eighth anniversary had recently passed almost unnoticed, and that morning, Ben and I had again fought bitterly over nothing on the way to hospital rounds. And again, I found myself questioning whether the little, lethal cruelties we inflicted on each other were worth the diminishing moments of peace and comfort we found together.

A voice said, "Terribly serious, isn't he? Like he's been at it for years."

I'd started and turned questioningly to the man who would become my lover. From his table, he gestured in the direction of the boy, who'd emerged from the kitchen and was ordering drinks from the bar. I nodded and smiled.

"How old do you think he is?" I asked.

"Ah, fourteen at the most, I'd say," he mused softly, then added with mock gravity, "Can't be much more yourself, can you?"

I laughed aloud and realized how rarely I'd been laughing lately.

"Thirty going on fifty," I said.

"Ah, come now, woman! It can't be all that bad."

After a moment of silence, his face fell, and he added soberly to himself, "Look who's talking. Of course it can be that bad."

We stared at each other, momentarily defenseless, then he said simply, "May I come and join you?"

The phone rings, and I find myself wondering where and when it will all end. How many times can we go flying across an ocean on flimsy excuses?

I pick up the receiver and hear the clerk say, "Dr. Bene-tar, we've got a real whopper for you down here. An eighty-three-year-old pearl the police just brought in."

The emergency room seems fairly quiet this morning for the surgeons and medical interns. An orderly mops up a small pool of blood in one of the empty cubicles, and the doctors on call lounge with their feet up, reading newspapers. A small portable radio in the corner announces another oldie but goodie, and the Everly Brothers start singing "Wake Up Little Susie." Two white-starched nurses rearrange a medication drawer. Harry, the emergency-room clerk, sticks his prematurely balding head around the door of his glassed-in office and says with a slightly effeminate lisp, "Well, if it isn't the shrink of the day. How about a couple of Librium for your good old uncle Harry? It's quiet now, but my nose tells me it's gonna be a helluva day."

"Just behave yourself and tell me where you've hidden my patient."

"She's in the back with the cops. A little old black lady as strong as an ox. It took two of them to carry her in here."

The chunky hospital security guard looks up from his crossword puzzle: "Hiya, gorgeous! Startin' in early today, aren't they?"

"Looks like it, Hank."

"If you want a nice break, you could take me next. See, I got this terrible crush on this beautiful lady doctor and she don't even know I exist. It's got so bad, I can't sleep nights anymore." He looks over at Harry and winks, and their laughter follows me down the hall.

Two enormous policemen are standing outside Room 135, three doors from the office marked *Emergency Psychiatry*. I notice that one of them is missing a few buttons from his jacket and the other has a long, red scratch near his left eye and shoeprints on his pants legs. Behind them, through the half-open door, I see a frail-looking, elderly black woman probably not more than four feet tall, sitting demurely in a flower-print dress with her hands in her lap, reading the Bible. I try to suppress a smile and say as evenly as possible, "Hello, officers, I'm Dr. Benetar. Can you tell me something about this lady?"

They both start to talk at once, and finally the one with

the missing buttons, Officer Smathers, explains that the woman, Miss Hettie Small, was throwing bottles and cans out her window on the fourteenth floor of an s.r.o. (single-room-occupancy) hotel and spitting and cursing at the pedestrians below. When the management tried to intervene, she barricaded the door of her room with the bed and continued her tirade. By the time the police arrived, the street was littered with broken glass and debris, but no one had been hurt. They forced open the door and found Miss Small cursing and talking to herself.

"Looks like she gave you a little trouble," I manage to say with a straight face.

"Yeah, well, she's a lot stronger than she looks, ma'am. Doctor. I'd advise you to be very careful."

I thank them and ask that one of them stay with me for the time being. Officer Smathers volunteers. We walk cautiously into the room, but there is no sign that the woman has noticed. Her lips move silently as she reads her holy book.

"Miss Small?"

She looks up with a beatific toothless smile, her close-cropped white hair not unlike a halo, and she says sweetly, "Yes . . . ?"

I introduce myself and she gently takes my hand and offers, "Very pleased to meet you, I'm sure."

Officer Smathers is aghast.

I suggest that we move into my office, which is more comfortable, and she thanks me and gets up to follow, steadying herself on the arm of the chair. She appears very frail indeed. The other astounded policeman excuses himself to return to duty, and she shakes his hand, too, and says she is delighted to have made his acquaintance.

He rubs the scratch on his cheek and mumbles, "Likewise, I'm sure," then walks off down the corridor shaking his head.

Officer Smathers and Hettie sit down on the blue studio

couch, and I pull the swivel chair away from the desk and draw it closer to them.

"How are you feeling, Miss Small?"

"Jus' fine, honey, jus' fine." She begins to rock back and forth very slightly.

"Do you know where you are?"

"Why, of course!" she says indignantly. "In West End General Hospital!"

"That's right. I just wanted to make sure you knew—"

"Well, of course I know! And I'll tell you sumpin' else you gonna ask me, too. Today's date is November sixteenth, Thursday. An' the Presidents before Nixon was Johnson and Kennedy and before him Ike an' as far back as you wanna go. . . . So there!" She resumes her rocking.

"Sounds like you've been around. Who else has asked you those questions?"

"Oh, doctors all over the place—different times, different places. Bellevue, Manhattan State, Pilgrim State, Rockland State. You name it, I been there."

"When was the last time?"

"Oh, I dunno. Maybe three, four years ago. Ain't nothin' wrong with me, you understan'. I jus' goes there sometime to he'p out."

"Oh. Miss Small, how old are you these days?"

"I'm eighty-three years old and I'm sixteen months' pregnant."

Officer Smathers edges away a few inches.

"I see. Does that have anything to do with why you got so upset today?"

"Upset? I weren't upset! Who says I were? I was jus' mindin' my own business and readin' the Lord's book." She opens the Bible and starts rocking harder.

"Well, the hotel manager where you live and the police said—"

She interrupts me loudly. "They crazy! I don't care what

they say. Disgustin', pickin' on a poh woman who might have a baby any time now. . . ."

I give her some time to settle down and fish in my handbag for a package of peppermints. Both she and Officer Smathers accept one.

"May I call you Hettie?"

"Why, of course, honey," she answers, smiling solicitously again.

"Well, Hettie, it seems you were throwing bottles down on people's heads today. Do you remember that?"

"Well, lemme think now, lemme think a minute. . . ."

She drifts into an absolute silence and seems to have forgotten the question and her surroundings.

"Hettie?"

She looks up with a strange half-smile and says in a rapid staccato, "Ibble tat no krona deeb blaza too. Keeda ma snow ham child blap. Zoo me. Tasta rak lim danana baba mad."

Before this moment, I had only read in textbooks of the schizophrenic "word salad," and just the week before had heard a lecture about what a rarity it had become in the last fifteen or twenty years. Officer Smathers is still trying to decide if it was Hettie or his ears.

She sweetly and thoughtfully adds, "You understan', honey?"

I answer as gently as possible, "No, Hettie, I don't think I do."

"Oh, tha's all right, child. It's all in the Bible. An' God provides for sinners and saints alike."

I excuse myself and check the register to see if we have beds available. Otherwise, Hettie Small will have to be sent elsewhere, and elsewhere is often bad news. The city hospitals have no upper limit on beds and cannot refuse to take a patient in obvious need of hospitalization, even if there is no room. The resultant overcrowding creates its own special brand of dehumanization in a psychiatric facility, and ironically, a patient's sense of isolation often grows more intense there. West End General, a medium-size "voluntary" hospital, is limited to about fifty psychiatric beds on its four inpatient psychiatric floors. The atmosphere is unhospital-like and human, the staffing is for the most part excellent, and the care is well above average.

And today, Hettie Small is lucky. We have space for her. By chance, she has beaten a system that from my unsophisticated point of view has been overwhelmed by its problems and thus far has responded with something equivalent to a Band-Aid.

During a series of lectures in medical school, we had been told that the group of drugs known as the "major tranquilizers" had recently revolutionized hospital psychiatry. On the proper medication, patients who previously had been locked away for years in back wards, tied in straitjackets, or subdued in cold-water packs were now able to be treated and returned to the community in a matter of months or even weeks. A comparative statistical survey of the length of hospital stay in 1945, 1955, 1965, and 1970 had been circulated among us, and we had been optimistic and impressed.

As a medical student in Ireland, my rotation through psychiatry had not been long enough to get a sense of how this worked in practice, and I lost contact with my patients after they were discharged. I do vaguely remember wondering about cultural differences and whether doctors back in the states were as impressed with the results of medication. Back in New York, I had found my internship too pressured with medical and surgical concerns to explore the question further, and I was only vaguely aware that my psychiatric colleagues were indeed using large doses of phenothiazine tranquilizers like Thorazine, Stelazine, Prolixin, and Mellaril on their psychotic patients.

The few books I managed to read during my intern year without falling asleep from exhaustion had already begun to hint at problems resulting from a too heavily medication-oriented approach, but it was not until my psychiatric residency that I came to fully appreciate certain aspects of what I might well call the "Hettie Small syndrome."

I glance over at her helping herself to another peppermint. What they told us in medical school is true enough in its own way. No more twenty-year hospitalizations, no cold-water packs, no padded cells, and only an occasional straitjacket in particularly violent, acute situations until the patient can be properly medicated. Certainly an improvement, but by no means the miraculous "solution" it was supposed to be.

Hettie smiles to herself. By now, her "syndrome" has become all too familiar to me. For whatever the reasons, and they are doubtless multiple, Hettie Small has been psychotic most of her life. When she or her younger counterparts present themselves to the West End General emergency room, they may be admitted for treatment if there is bed space available and if they live within the boundaries of the hospital district. Partly because of the almost immediately observable chemical tranquilization, the law about length of stay permitted for indigent patients was changed during the last few years. West End General and other voluntary hospitals are now restricted to a time-limited treatment period of thirty days, unless the patient has special insurance or is independently wealthy. (The cost of a psychiatric hospital bed, apart from any tests or other treatment that may be required, is over $100 a day.) Under exceptional circumstances, which have yet to be clearly defined, the physician can apply for an additional thirty-day extension, and, very rarely, for a second extension of thirty days.

But ordinarily, at the end of a month, Hettie Small would either be discharged on her medication or she would be transferred to a state mental hospital, where she would most likely be more heavily medicated and then released as soon as she seemed even marginally tractable. In either case, she would eventually be returned to her environment, which in the case of the West End General area, is a community heavily populated by ex-mental hospital patients like her, addicts, prostitutes and pimps, impoverished minority groups, eccentrics, and a large group of isolated senior citizens. West End General has a department of community psychiatry that makes some effort at follow-up care; it has four or five on-site psychiatric team projects and a crisis-intervention team that takes referrals from anywhere within the densely populated hospital "catchment area," as the district outlined by the city is called. But for a variety of reasons, more often than not, the hospital loses touch with patients like Hettie Small. The sheer numbers of people with which it has to deal are alone untenable. Then it must contend with a jungle of bureaucratic red tape, a basically unsympathetic social and political system, and its own internal squabbles. Although the aim is toward cohesiveness and continuity of care, in practice such a scheme is nearly impossible to implement, except for a tiny percentage of the people requiring assistance.

And so, on her discharge from the hospital, a Hettie Small is generally armed with prescriptions and bottles of major tranquilizers. After a variable amount of time back in her single-room-occupancy hotel and dreary, dangerous environment, when left to herself, she usually stops taking her medication, again becomes agitated and disruptive, and is brought back, or occasionally walks in voluntarily to another emergency room.

In summary, the cycle is: West End General Hospital emergency room to its own inpatient service or Bellevue's; medication and, depending on the hospital and the individual doctor involved, maybe some attempts at psychotherapy, which cannot accomplish much in a thirty-day period; if little improvement, transfer to a state hospital; more medication; eventual discharge to the same environment; without follow-up care, loss of interest in others, and loss of self-interest, including failure to take medication; return to West End General emergency room, and so on.

Occasionally, a follow-up system works; or a zealous psychiatric resident or social worker or community mental health worker will doggedly stick with a Hettie Small and attempt to work out a long-term treatment plan for her, aimed at some minimal kind of satisfactory reintegration. But that is the exception, and within our current social system it is a drop in the ocean. For the most part, we have settled for a legion of heavily tranquilized, psychotically troubled people, who periodically make the rounds of the various hospitals.

In my own limited experience, I have found the major tranquilizers invaluable in helping someone through a period of acute psychotic stress and terror. When that has passed, I think that, with some chronic exceptions, drugs are less important and even inhibitory at times. It is difficult to make any sustained, meaningful contact with someone whose ability to feel and relate has been compromised by a chemical.

I do not presume to know all the causes for or answers to the "Hettie Small syndrome." But I suspect that some kind of resolution lies within individuals, in their concepts of relatedness, in their notions of self-and-social concern and appreciation. As it relates to me, I guess I see one of my major roles in my work as an attempt to help people acquire or regain a sense of their own autonomy.

Hettie has begun to rock back and forth holding the Bible over her belly. Officer Smathers is picking his nose.

"Hettie, how would you feel about coming back into the hospital for a little while?"

The rocking stops, the smile fades. Hettie looks somewhere at the wall above my head and starts shouting, "Fuck! Shit! Piss! Balls, bellies, and tits! You cock-suckin' bitch, I'm not goin' into no hospital. No, ma'am!"

The policeman's ruddy cheeks are scarlet. The expletives continue, and I wonder at what point in my training they began to seem commonplace to me. My indifference to them and to a series of nightmarish scenes in the e.r. is probably highly suspect. It shields and consoles me and helps me get through the twenty-four-hour period. But it can be a double-edged sword, treacherous, a form of self-betrayal and a disservice to the people I see. Because if I allow myself to become too complacent, I may stop asking questions one day.

Hettie's shouting has diminished and become a kind of rhythmical incantation. She has begun to tremble. She has also obviously begun to hallucinate and punctuates her stream of profanities with brief, unintelligible asides to someone she calls Hector.

I try a desperate ploy to reduce her increasing agitation and fear of hospitalization.

"Hettie, what does your doctor say about the baby?"

The question gets through.

"What do you mean? I ain't got no doctor."

"Well, don't you think you should have? Someone in your delicate condition ought to be properly cared for—maybe even in a hospital at this point."

"Yeah, maybe so—never thought of it that way. What do you think, Hector? . . ." She listens thoughtfully, nods, and then asks, "Can I get vitamins and stuff if I come into this place?"

"Of course. You'll have your own doctor assigned to take care of you."

It's a dirty trick but it works. And it's better than another button scene with Officer Smathers. Before she has time to change her mind, we escort her up to Castle 10.

On the ward, Officer Smathers remarks, "Christ, what happened to the hospital? This place looks like a Holiday Inn!"

He looks in wonder at the reproductions of famous paintings, the utilitarian wall-to-wall carpeting, the bookshelves and stereo system just visible in the day room, the cheap but comfortable furniture, and the casual dress of the staff and patients.

"Yes, I guess it's a bit of a shock if you're not prepared for it," I say to the baffled policeman, who is standing, hands on hips, shaking his head. "We like to think it's easier to start getting yourself together in an atmosphere like this. There are a few other places around like it. Maybe you'd like to stay and look around for a while?"

He breaks into an embarrassed grin, "No, ma'am! No disrespect intended, doctor, but not on your life! Thanks, but no thanks! I've already left my partner alone too long, anyway."

Jane, a nurse's aide, comes out to greet us in jeans and a bright red poncho, wearing a new Afro wig. She invites Hettie to sit down so she can take her blood pressure.

I turn and thank Officer Smathers for his time and patience. Relieved to be dismissed, his parting remark to me is meant good-naturedly enough.

"Well, I sure have had an eyeful today. Hope you don't mind my saying so, doctor, but it's a little hard to tell who's who around here. Whatever happened to the little men in the white coats?"

He laughs as the elevator door closes in front of him. A thin young man standing by the window spits on the floor. He turns to the room and says, "Fascist pigs! All of you." Then he bows three times and adds, "Thank you. Thank you, ladies and gentlemen," and resumes his vigil over the street below.

Jane answers the phone in the nurses' station and comes out to tell me there's another patient downstairs in the emergency room. I begin to give her a brief rundown on Hettie, which is interrupted by a movement in the corner of my vision.

"Jane, if you want to save yourself a lot of work, you might escort Miss Small to the ladies' room."

Jane looks, utters a brief "Oh, no!" and runs. Hettie has rather unceremoniously pulled down her underpants and hiked up her flower-print dress to defecate in a potted palm. With a speed and dexterity that come only from years of experience with such episodes, Jane deftly propels Hettie Small around the corner into the bathroom.

The second person to see me is somewhere outside in the waiting area. I take the *Emergency Room Record Form—XIAA-32* from the psychiatrists' box, where Harry has neatly typed in: "Victor Nelson. *Age:* 32. *Address:* 48–55 38th Street, Long Island City, Queens. *Complaint:* Wants to see psychiatrist. *Mode of arrival:* Walked in."

"Dr. Cohen!" a nurse calls anxiously somewhere behind me, "Code Zero coming in!" Ned Cohen comes running out of the john, zipping up his fly, shirttail hanging out of his pants. Aides and other nurses appear from nowhere and start readying equipment in the room for cardiac emergencies. The ambulance has come screaming in and screeches to a halt. An elderly man is wheeled in on a stretcher and is quickly appraised by Ned, who throws an Ambu bag at the nurse and mutters, "Get him ventilated, Sue, he's cyanotic as hell!"

Ned, who is just over five feet tall, then jumps up on the stretcher and kneeling beside the man's chest commences external cardiac massage. I hear a rib snap and remember the feeling of it under my hands when I was the one pumping on the sternum. The curious trio is wheeled to the cardiac cubicle by an aide, and a curtain is pulled incompletely across the door. In the gap, I can see an intern starting an I.V. and aides hooking up EKG leads.

I open the door to the waiting room, which is beginning to fill up. In the corner, a drunk snores loudly, his gray stubble clotted with dried food and blood. A young, pretty Puerto Rican mother tries to comfort a crying baby. Holding her head in her hands, an obese black woman moans and mumbles under her breath. An expensively dressed young couple sit nervously staring at the clerk waiting to be called; the man jumps up when I open the door.

"Mr. Nelson?" I inquire.

The man shakes his head and sits down again, disappointed.

I look around questioningly at Harry, who points to the phone booth. An athletic-looking man with a square jaw and all-American good looks is having an animated and apparently unsatisfactory telephone conversation. He slams the receiver down, opens the door, and remains seated there, biting his knuckles in deep thought.

"Mr. Nelson?" I repeat.

The man looks up and I notice that there are heavy, dark pouches under his eyes. As he comes toward me, he weaves almost imperceptibly.

"I'm Victor Nelson," he says importantly, "and who are you?"

"I'm Dr. Benetar, the psychiatrist. Would you follow me, please?"

"By all means, lady doctor, lead the way—unbelievable chic."

We pass the half-open curtain, where the cardiac patient is being defibrillated. Electrode handles on the chest, button pressed, body in brief spasm, silence, and then inertia. Mr. Nelson gets a quick glimpse of the last second of activity.

"Hey, doc, what's going on in there?"

"A man had a heart attack. They're trying to resuscitate him."

"Glad you told me. For a minute, I thought it was Dr. Terror's House of Horrors."

He laughs nervously, then tries to look jaunty and unconcerned. In the office, he lapses into a strained silence. He asks if I mind if he smokes, and I notice his hands trembling slightly as he lights his cigarette. Despite his Charles Atlas come-on, he has obviously lost a lot of weight recently. There is an extra, hand-punched hole in his somewhat worn leather belt. His wool slacks and open sport shirt are good quality, but both are soiled at the cuffs. Shoes are scuffed and dull. What must be a naturally ruddy complexion has a funny, grayish-yellow tinge. He takes a deep breath, exhales, and says with a false bravado, "Doc, I'm in a little trouble right now, but you look like you might be able to help."

I wait.

He begins to look a little less assured and goes on, "You see, I'm a little down on my luck these days. Actually, I've been out of a job since the summer. I worked as a lifeguard at Jones Beach—good at it, too. Saved a couple of people. I guess you might call me a sort of natural athlete. Used to play quarterback in college. . . ."

His words trail off and he begins to fumble with the ash tray.

"How have you been living since the lifeguard job? It's November, now."

"Oh, I manage. I manage okay," he says too quickly. "Yeah, I get around all right."

"Then what kind of trouble are you in?"

"I'm coming to that. . . ."

Then the words tumble out all over each other. "It's my nerves, doctor. I just feel like I might fall apart. Couldn't you give me some pills to tide me over? I really could use a good night's sleep. Could you let me have some Seconal or Librium or Quaalude, maybe?"

The light begins to dawn, and I feel suddenly tired and depressed. I had been thrown off by the square jaw and football-hero bit, and hadn't really connected up the usually obvious clues.

He mistakes my silence for a kind of acquiescence and adds hungrily, "If you could give me a little paraldehyde right now, it would be easier to sit and talk to you."

"Paraldehyde??"

"Yeah. I've had a sort of drinking problem lately, and paraldehyde always helps me stop. I'm not drunk now, of course. Just a bit jittery. Could you get some for me?" The desperation is now out in the open.

"Mr. Nelson, if I'm going to be able to help you at all, you're going to have to tell me exactly what you're taking these days—how much alcohol, what pills, how many and how often."

"Really, doc, you gotta believe me. I'm clean now. It's just my nerves, really. I might go into d.t.'s, though, if you don't get me some paraldehyde."

A year ago, when I first started assignments on call in the emergency room, he might have succeeded in conning me to give him anything he wanted. The city has a legion of alcoholics and drug abusers who regularly make the rounds of hospital emergency rooms looking for naive beginning residents whom they can manipulate or emotionally intimidate into helping them perpetuate their addiction.

"Mr. Nelson, you live in Queens, right? How is it that you decided to come to a Manhattan hospital for help?"

"Well, I—they were too busy at the hospital near me, and a friend who was in a car accident last year told me to come here. He said you get really good treatment here. I—doc, I'm really in bad shape. Will you please give me something, anything, please?"

He has begun to sweat profusely and the tremor has grown more marked.

"How much alcohol have you had today?"

"None. I couldn't afford it."

"Yesterday?"

"Quart and a half of whiskey."

"That your average?"

"When I'm drinking, yes. But I haven't been drinking lately, except for yesterday. Honest."

"Pills?"

"Three twenty-five-milligram Librium this morning. It was all I had left."

"What else?"

"Nothing—just a little English Leather after shave. Really, doctor. In the past, sure, I took just about everything, I guess—ups, downs, junk, acid, you name it. But nothing lately, except what I just told you."

"Then why are you in such a mess?"

"It's just my nerves, I keep telling you. Jesus, doctor, give me something, will you?!"

I pick up the phone and call one of the nurses at the front desk and ask to have Mr. Nelson checked out by the medical resident.

"And give him ten milligrams of Valium also, would you?"

"Sure thing."

"By the way, how did that cardiac arrest turn out?"

"Didn't make it."

When I hang up, Victor Nelson says, "Ten milligrams of Valium! Christ, that's not enough! What about paraldehyde instead?"

"Look, Mr. Nelson, I'll talk to you again after you've had a medical examination and we can both be sure you're not going into d.t.'s. In the meantime, I think ten milligrams of Valium should hold you."

He is about to argue further when the nurse enters with his medication and leads him out of the room. As they leave, I take out a directory for the listing of the hospital in his area of Queens and call the psychiatric resident on duty.

After ten minutes of paging and unfathomable, unavoidable, infuriating, hospital-operator bureaucracy, a gentle

Indian voice finally answers: "Hello, this is Dr. Jawahli speaking."

"Dr. Jawahli, this is Dr. Benetar at West End General. I have a man here in our emergency room from your area who looks as though he may need hospitalization and probably detoxification. His name is Victor Nelson and—"

A pained protest that is hard to associate with the voice that answered the phone cuts me off: "Oh, no! You have Victor Nelson there? Oh, God help us, not again!"

"I take it you know him?"

When the doctor regains some of his former composure, he tells me that Victor Nelson is a well-known paraldehyde addict and alcoholic who has been in and out of their hospital at least eight times in the past two years. He eloped from his most recent hospitalization ten days ago, at which time he was under the care, coincidentally, of Dr. Jawahli. His many detoxifications from paraldehyde, alcohol, and whatever else he happened to have been on prior to each admission, had been exceptionally difficult to manage, for if the withdrawal regimen were not gradual enough, Victor would become paranoid and violent, or if they misjudged, as they had on one previous occasion, and prescribed too much medication, he lapsed into coma. Presumably because of his appearance, he had managed to get himself hired for various odd jobs in the last couple of years, including the one as a lifeguard in the summer, though it lasted only a week and a half. He kept his paraldehyde in a thermos next to him on the lifeguard stand. When his colleagues questioned him about the overpowering, noxious odor of the liquid, he would explain that it was a special medication he had had to take since childhood for his liver. The job ended one day when he swallowed a little too much and went staggering around the beach insulting the bathers.

Reluctantly, Dr. Jawahli agrees to accept the patient in transfer when he has been "medically cleared." I hang up thinking what the term has come to mean in a busy New York City hospital emergency room unable to handle the numbers of physical, social, and emotional problems that pass through its doors. Theoretically, someone who has been medically cleared has had a complete physical checkup for his complaint, sometimes an X ray or some blood tests if they seem called for. If, after careful consideration, he has been found to have no *acutely* life-threatening illness or any problem serious enough to require immediate hospitalization, he is declared medically clear and healthy enough to be discharged, or transferred, or, if necessary, referred for treatment on an outpatient basis.

In practice, there are a number of people who, largely for reasons of expediency (such as facilities inadequate to cope with their multidimensional problems), tend to be rather superficially passed over and medically cleared after, at the most, a quick, unseeing "heart-and-lung-check." The bulk of these people tend to be chronic down-and-outers, including various drug abusers like Victor, and an army of neglected, unwanted senior citizens who make their way to the hospital from various dingy welfare-hotel rooms or nursing homes. Often they have legitimate, serious, medical problems, but there is simply no place to put them. So unless they are almost in immediate danger of dying, these people are usually returned to the places from whence they come to deteriorate at varying rates of speed to a point where hospitalization is unavoidable. Or they just die.

Medical clearance for Victor Nelson prior to his transfer is largely a matter of formality, except for the possibility of impending d.t.'s, which have a high mortality rate and would call for immediate hospital care.

I fill out the transfer forms and think about getting some lunch after discussing the arrangements I have made with Victor. I find him sitting on the edge of a stretcher in one of the cubicles, watching Ned Cohen examine his chest. He is bare to the waist and slouches limply forward as Ned

listens with his stethoscope. There is something patheti-
cally bizarre in the contrast between the tiny, confident,
slightly manic young doctor, who comes on at times like a
Jewish Mickey Rooney, and the patient, who towers over
him, even sitting down, now having abandoned all attempts at bravado and looking incredibly haggard and lost.

"Okay, sir," Ned says, tucking the stethoscope in his
pocket, "you can put your shirt back on now."

He looks up and sees me standing in the doorway.

"Oh, hi, Judy. He's essentially okay. Liver's down about
five centimeters and his pressure and pulse are up a bit, but
nothing to write home about. Not impending d.t.'s, anyway. I don't know what you're planning for him, but if he
has to sit around awhile waiting for transfer or something,
you might ask the nurses to get another set of vital signs on
him before he leaves." He is out the door before I can reply
or thank him.

I turn to Victor Nelson, who is having some trouble
buttoning his shirt.

He looks at me worriedly. "What'd he just say in plain
English?"

"That you're slowly poisoning your liver with all that
stuff you're taking, but that you're reasonably all right for
the time being. You're not going into d.t.'s this time, anyway."

He nods and tries, "Valium did help a little, doc, but I'm
still pretty jumpy. Some paraldehyde or somethin' might
just do the trick."

"Mr. Nelson, I just talked with Dr. Jawahli."

"Oh, no." He looks guiltily away. "He tell you everything?"

"Pretty much, I guess."

"Well, that's that, I suppose."

He sighs and eases down off the stretcher.

"Thanks for your help, doc. Guess I'll be going, now."

"Hold on a minute, Victor. You really don't look like

you're in much shape to go anywhere. How about another try at detox and hospitalization?"

"That an order?"

"Nope. I can't force you to do anything you don't want to do, unless you're going to go out and kill yourself or somebody else. That's the law, and by now, I'm sure you know that as well as I do."

"Hah! I'm not smart enough to do anything simple like that. My way is gonna take years. . . ."

"You know, one of these times, if you can find some motivation somewhere, the detox might work, with a little professional help."

"Nice try, doc." He puts on his coat. "Thanks, really. I really do appreciate it. But I got a few more things I want to look into first and some phone calls to make. I can see Dr. Jawahli and his friends anytime. Well, see ya."

He almost manages to square his shoulders and walk away looking unconcerned.

I throw the transfer papers in the wastepaper basket, close my mind, and fill out the remainder of the emergency-room record form as he disappears out the door. In the appropriate spaces, I write: "Victor Nelson, 32 . . . Emotional Illness; Multiple Drug Abuse. . . ."

Total time in the emergency room by the punch clock, forty-six minutes; emergency room fee, $19.50; Valium tablet, 15¢; disposition: Out. Then a short psychiatric note on the carbon copy "blue sheet" for the confidential use of future on-call psychiatric residents, to be filed away with several thousand others in the metal cabinet in the corner.

"Fuck it," I say to an empty room and decide to get some lunch. Had I not learned to block out, on some level, the worry I would have felt about him several months ago, I probably would have quit my residency.

I manage to knock over the ash tray with three of Victor's half-smoked butts on the way out of the room. Seeing the ashes and crumpled stubs on the floor recalls a time when I was a medical student in Dublin, and a huge laborer was brought in by ambulance after a four-car collision at one of the major crossroads. He had sustained multiple fractures and injuries, and the most ominous sign was a quiet stream of blood and cerebral fluid oozing slowly from his left ear. He was dead in half an hour. I helped the aides search his pockets for identification. In the pocket of his plaid wool shirt were a package of cigarettes and some partially smoked butts he must have been saving for future use. A priest was administering the last rites. Despite my resolve to maintain a clinical objectivity, when I saw the cigarettes and realized that they were more intact and viable than he was, I dropped them and watched them scatter across the tile floor. Someone took me to my room and muttered something about how I would get used to these things in time. Then I slept for twelve hours.

I shake my head to dispel the memory and inadequately start to clean up the mess I have just made. There is a sound at the door, and I look up to see Luke, one of the black aides, beaming down at me in a spotless white uniform, which means that he has just begun his shift.

"Well, Dr. Benetar, I hear that psychiatrists are up to some strange things these days, but this particular form of therapy is new to me. What do you call it?"

"Encounter with Ashes before Lunch."

He laughs and says he'll see me later.

The large cafeteria is crowded but not yet at its lunchtime peak. I glance by habit at the menu on the wall:

Chicken Gumbo soup
Split Pea soup

Italian macaroni
Salisbury steak

Scallops
Broiled lamb chop
Hamburger
Hot dog

Stewed tomatoes
Creamed spinach
Carrots and peas

As usual, everything looks more or less the same color and consistency, and I vaguely wonder which label matches up with which food on the steam table as I pass on to the salad counter and sandwich line.

Joe Lorenzo nearly crashes into me with his tray, talking over his shoulder to another medical resident about a diagnosis. His usual nonstop staccato is barely interrupted by the collision. Joe's resemblance to Groucho Marx is even more striking as he hurriedly whispers under his moustache to me, "Hiya, gorgeous! How are you? Wouldn't need a good lay, would you?"

"Doesn't everyone?"

"Yeah, but me more than most people. Gotta keep the batteries charged to take care of the sick and dying. You look beautiful, by the way. How's the shrink business?"

Without waiting for an answer, he winks and continues his conversation with the other resident, ". . . yeah, Christ, Ray, I really thought I had it nailed till I saw that second chest film . . . and the old guy's B.U.N. shot up to sixty-four almost overnight."

The large main eating area is jammed with aides, nurses, auxiliary personnel, and several doctors. Seeing no one I know well enough to join except Joe and Ray, I make my way to the semi-partitioned-off corner marked *Doctors Only*, hoping to find a table, but irritated again at its exclusiveness. I guess one of the stronger things I have come to feel since I got my M.D. is that it could be valuable for everyone concerned for doctors to make some effort at reducing their rather mystical separateness from other people. To set one-self up as something a little beyond ordinary human vul-nerabilities, or to allow others to do so, seems to me an invitation to unreasonable expectations and a blind, unquestioning dependency that at the least can be mislead-ing, and at the worst, dangerous.

As usual, there are free tables in the "Doctors Only" section. Three other psychiatric residents see me and ges-ture to the fourth seat.

Larry Marks looks even more depressed than usual, and I remember hearing that he and his girl friend Betty have split up again for the third time this year. He pulls the chair out for me and manages a half-smile.

"Hi, Judy. You on call today?"

"Yes, why?"

"One of the patients I've been seeing twice a week since her discharge from the hospital in June is starting to de-compensate. I told her to come in to the e.r. if she began feeling suicidal again. Don't know if she will, but it's a possibility. Her name is Grace Blackwell."

He pauses and takes a bite of his hamburger, chewing thoughtfully.

Alan Goldberg, one of Larry's best friends, tugs charac-teristically at his beard and says half jokingly, "Your depression catching, Larry?"

"Don't laugh, Al. I think that may be one of the reasons why she's slipping. I just haven't been there for her."

"Christ, Larry! You never let up on yourself. Why don't you let your patient in on the fact that you're a little down right now. It might make her feel like she's got something in common with you, or allow her to acknowledge that you're both human beings."

"Oh, come on, Al!"

"Oh, sorry, I forgot for a minute that you're going the orthodox route these days. God forbid you should be a real live human being. Who knows what would happen?"

"Just because you can't understand the basic principles of analytically oriented therapy, don't go around knocking the people who can."

Listening to this all-too-familiar exchange between Larry and Al, a quick, recurrent question flits across my awareness. To oversimplify the matter, the basic issue between the two friends is that Larry has a rather classical analytic approach to patients and has, in fact, begun training at a recognized orthodox analytic school. This implies that, among other things, he will have to train himself to be as impersonal as possible in a therapeutic situation, so that his feelings and personality will not intrude themselves on the patient's difficulties.

Al, on the other hand, has pursued a course of study which believes that however objective one trains oneself to be, the patient will inevitably pick up, from various verbal and nonverbal clues, information about Al the person and his feelings in certain situations. With this as a basic premise, Al would train himself to utilize his own personality and feelings at times when his reactions seemed therapeutically useful, while identifying them to the patient as *his* and himself as human, vulnerable, and responsive.

Volumes of psychiatric literature have been written about this difference in approach and the various schools that have developed as offshoots of one or the other. All are impressive and convincing in their own ways. The question that I cannot help wondering about has to do with the choice each therapist makes for himself. Is it not a statement about the person behind the therapist? I find it difficult to believe that in a profession with so many variables, so many immeasurable factors, in essence, a field that seems to me relatively unscientific, the choice of approach has to do with reason alone.

Although at this point in my training I cannot be certain

what direction I will choose, it is certainly clear to me from my limited experience with patients, and also in my life, that there is a value in being spontaneous and open. The art in psychiatry appears to me to be in learning when and where and how to exercise a degree of control over that spontaneity in the patient's interest.

Al and Larry have begun to grow more heated in their argument, and I can see my lunch break dissolving into an endless theoretical hassle.

Carol Saks, sitting across from me, makes a face and diplomatically tries to intervene.

"Would you two guys mind if we didn't talk shop for five minutes? I've just come from two hours of conferences and I've really had it."

Alan perks up. "Oh, did you go to Lehmann's conference, Carol? I couldn't make it, and I really wanted to go. What did he talk about?"

Forgetting her request not to talk shop, Carol, who is in advanced training for child psychiatry, begins to outline the seminar on autistic children.

My interest is captured initially by her reference to the work of an Australian woman whose approach is new to me and whose results thus far have been exceptional, although there has not been enough time for follow-up to confirm her success.

Autistic children are among the most difficult people to treat in psychiatry. They are completely self-absorbed, will not relate to parents or others, often will not eat, except for rather bizarre "food fetishes," and spend much of their time performing seemingly meaningless, stereotyped, repetitive movements, such as rocking for hours at a time. Despite the mountain of theoretical speculation that has been written about these children, few therapists have had any real success in treating them.

Carol has been clearly impressed by the Australian woman's work. "Her approach sounds so simple, it's almost ridiculous," she says enthusiastically. "Lehmann read us part of one of her papers. . . . Want me to go on?"

We all nod and she continues, "Well, for example, she decided that step one was to make certain these children were genuinely autistic, that is, that they were not deaf, or brain damaged, or in any measureable way biochemically or genetically defective. Hospitalization and a complete work-up is required for that part.

"Then, once the diagnosis of uncomplicated autism had been made, step two was to get these kids properly nourished. She mentioned one kid who subsisted on a diet of crackers and orange rind. If I can remember a quote from her, 'How can one even consider dealing with more complicated problems when the child isn't taking in the proper nourishment?' "

Carol pauses and shakes her head.

"God," she says, "Leave it to the British to be practical! This woman's originally from England somewhere. So anyway, the way she went about tackling the food problem was to move the child's entire family into a special wing of the hospital for a while, so that it could be as close to the home environment as possible for all of them. Then, because the process she'd devised turned out in the early stages of her work to be too painful for the mother to participate in, she would send the mother away at mealtimes, and she herself would offer the child a well-balanced meal. Of course, the child would ignore her for a variable length of time—usually days, she said, but her longest case was well over a week. The food, after being rejected, would then be taken away, and other family activities would go on. By the way, fluids would be available to the child at all times.

"Anyway, even with the mother not being involved in the feeding process, it would be painful for her to watch, because, with almost no nourishment at all, these kids would start looking like hell, crying a lot, sometimes getting weak, cranky, and generally miserable. Often the mother would be tempted to give in and give him his crackers and orange rind or whatever. But since the therapist is in constant touch with the family, she intervenes and explains the rationale and prevents the mother from relenting."

Carol pauses and takes a bite of cold macaroni before she continues, "I think she said this is the most difficult period for everybody—patient, family, and therapist. After that, it gets better and better. But at any rate, there comes a time when the child finally accepts and eats the food that is offered him. In every case, so far. At this point, the therapist calls in the mother and begins to involve her in the feeding process. Naturally, the mother's overjoyed that the kid's eating and gives him a lot of affection, praise, and general reinforcement for what he's accomplished. Then it's the mother who begins to offer the kid his meals, and when his new eating pattern has been firmly established, the therapist begins a series of exercises to deal with the other problems, like communication. She begins with an exercise to establish eye contact with the mother, in play form, and works up to a meaningful verbal and physical exchange with her and other members of the family. In time, they're discharged to a day center for continuation of treatment. Other people who have learned from her are claiming over eighty percent success rates, but she's more modest and responds with something like 'time will tell.' "

Larry interrupts with a question about the psychodynamic implications of some of the interactions, to which Carol responds, "Later, Larry. Lehmann got into that, too, but it's too much to go into now. I took some notes you can have if you want; they're up in my locker."

She continues to outline some of the other exercises and follow-up treatment that is managed on a day-center or other outpatient basis. Larry sinks back into his own thoughts, and I manage to listen for about five minutes before my attention wanders.

From where I'm sitting, I have a good view of the rest of "Doctors Only," and I let my eyes drift around the other tables. Two attending physicians in their forties sit at the table nearest us, heavily engrossed in a discussion about land they're planning to buy in the Adirondacks. Beyond them is a group of obstetricians, as usual convulsed with laughter. One of them gets up and lifts his leg against the wall, presumably imitating a dog at a fire hydrant, says something I can't hear, and is greeted by renewed hysterics from his table, applause, and the sound of one of his colleagues choking on half-swallowed food. The long table in the middle of the area is occupied by about six surgical residents, some still in operating greens, no doubt discussing the morning's procedures. I can just make out snatches of dialogue: ". . . incredible woman must have weighed over two hundred pounds; just hundreds of bleeders in all that fat . . . took us half the morning to tie them off. . . ."

Someone responds loudly, "What've you got to complain about? I spent two hours disimpacting some old geezer. Can't believe anyone could contain so much shit—take me days to stop smelling it."

At the end of their table, I discover one of the surgical residents watching me watch them. Our eyes meet, and somehow the expression on my face makes him laugh gently to himself. I smile back at his warmth, and feel that there has been a rare moment of nonverbal exchange between two very different kinds of doctors. As in many hospitals, the atmosphere at West End General between psychiatrists and other physicians is cordial but somewhat strained. In the end, it comes down to individuals and what they think of each other, but in general, there is a notion that shrinks are either crazy themselves or don't know what they're doing, or that it's an easy profession where you can make a lot of money playing mental games. I guess I think that this attitude is partly from fear of what people will discover in themselves if they give up this notion, and partly, I suppose, it is as true of psychiatry as of any other field. Certainly, psychiatry is as open to charlatans and opportunists as any other branch of medicine, but I suspect that the attacks on it have been overdone. It makes a convenient scapegoat.

Alan puts his hand on my arm and says, "Judy, hello! Come back to us."

"I'm sorry, Alan, I wasn't listening. What did you say?"

"I asked if you still want me to cover for you from five to seven today."

"Yes, please, Alan. I have a shrink appointment, and then I have to go home and feed my cats."

"Okay, that's fine with me. Can you do the same for me next week? I'm on call Tuesday, and my shrink appointment's from two to three."

"Sure, I'm free then."

I go back for a second cup of coffee, and when I return to the table, the surgeons have left. We finish our lunch mostly in silence, broken by occasional banter, attempts at humor, and nondescript small talk. Larry and Alan are quietly annoyed with each other, and again I find myself thinking that if we were all less afraid of our own humanity, we'd have a lot to learn from each other and ourselves.

Carol and I exchange thoughts about why it has been relatively pleasant to work as women at West End General. Neither of us can decide to what extent the women's movement has influenced the hospital, because our acceptance has been so natural and unaffected from the beginning, with few exceptions. We had both considered that it might be that women are more easily accepted in psychiatry, a field known for its avant-garde thinking and ideas.

"Though, of course," Carol interjects, "there's the whole controversy about Freudian theory and how the notion of penis envy, for example, is a prime example of male chauvinism and helps reinforce the inferior position of women in our culture."

"True, but even in the days of Clara Thompson and Melanie Klein that was being questioned," I remind her, "And it seems to me that only the most rigidly Freudian analysts still strongly adhere to it."

Carol nods, then changes the subject, and I remember that she is herself having an internal struggle about how much orthodox Freudian theory she wants to accept. We share anecdotes from the days of our medical internships. Both of us had had a difficult time in different hospitals with colleagues, auxiliary staff, and patients. She laughs aloud at my description of a night on call in medicine when an army sergeant needed treatment for a boil on his buttock.

"I'm not taking my pants down for no woman, no matter how many degrees she has, and no matter how many white coats she wears or stethoscopes she carries!"

At a natural lull in the conversation, we all get up and collect our empty dishes. The portable beeper I carry in my pocket goes off as I deposit my tray on the conveyor belt to the kitchen, and I am paged for an extension that sounds familiar to me, but which I can't quite place.

Dr. White, one of the psychiatric administrators, answers my call. "Hi, Judy. Are you busy in the emergency room?"

"Not at the moment, Dr. White. I just finished lunch."

"Shame on you. Don't tell me you forgot about our appointment? We're all up here waiting for you. . . ."

"Oh, my god! I'm awfully sorry, Dr. White. I *was* busy this morning, and it just completely slipped my mind. I'll be right up."

I hang up and try to contain my increasing anxiety. I have neatly managed to keep four administrators, who are about to discuss my annual evaluation with me, waiting in the office of the head of the department for fifteen minutes so far. The elevator, naturally, is again up on one of the top floors and is interminably slow in coming down. I berate myself for being so upset. No adult, at this stage of the game, should be in such a state for forgetting an appointment. Unbelievably idiotic carryover from childhood.

On my way up, I have a quick painful memory of inventing imaginative stories about sick relatives and broken plumbing to explain away my chronic tardiness at school. More often than not, the real explanation had to do with stubbornly refusing to get out of bed in the morning and moving at a speed that was in inverse proportion to the anger and urgency in my mother's voice. Then after I'd missed the school bus, my stepfather would have to drive me, chastising all the way, with special emphasis on how "we deserve more respect and cooperation from you, young lady."

I would sit next to him and watch the skimpy trees along the road slip by, growing quietly more anxious about what I could say to the teacher that would sound convincing. It was somehow important to be liked and wanted at school.

I open the door to the administrative division. The secretary raises her eyebrows and tells me to go right in. Whatever conversation has been going on prior to my arrival stops abruptly when I enter. They are an incongruous bunch. The head of the department, Dr. Faulkner, is a brilliant, complicated man whom few people understand and most find difficult to get close to. With a characteristic explosive laugh, he once said in the same breath that there were never any answers to anything, but that he was at least fifty years ahead of his time anyway, "in my own way of saying that there are no answers, that is." Dr. Faulkner's chief delight in life is paradox, which he seems to find almost everywhere. This is naturally disturbing to people who like to find concrete resolutions to things, as do most psychiatrists. He is somewhat unpopular among enthusiastic, beginning psychiatric residents, who often enter their profession with a missionary zeal, hoping to "cure" most of their patients.

Dr. Faulkner's passion in life is "communication," and he has published widely in a rather avant-garde field known as "structural psychiatry." He rarely involves himself in house–staff affairs, except to lecture and do a few hours of supervision each week. Most of his time is spent seeing patients, doing administrative work, and writing papers and books on the theory of communication and language. When I enter, he looks up briefly from the papers he is shuffling on his desk, smiles, and invites me to sit down.

The others are more expressionless. Dr. Dunbar, a fairly orthodox Freudian analyst who conceals his personal inadequacy behind caustic sarcasms and frequent nebulous, impenetrable anecdotes which he, at least, seems to find amusing, glances deliberately at his watch as I walk in. He sits on a studio couch next to Dr. White, whose orientation in psychiatry is about as far from Freudian as you can get. Dr. White is a delightfully engaging homosexual, who relies heavily on medication and biophysical forms of therapy in the treatment of seriously disturbed patients. The little psychotherapy he employs is mostly supportive and rather simplistic.

The fourth administrative consultant is Dr. Schwartz, a young, bright, upper-middle-class Harvard graduate who did his psychiatric training in one of the better-known postgraduate centers. He tries hard to be eclectic and open-minded, but doesn't always manage. (But then, who does?) Dr. Schwartz always, as now, holds his head at a funny tilt when trying to appear noncommittal. The effect is sort of bird-listening-for-a-worm, but benign and welcoming.

Except for Dr. Dunbar, who constantly exudes hostility, the atmosphere is definitely not threatening.

I apologize for keeping them waiting and take the remaining seat, which is across from Dr. White, who looks as though he may do most of the talking. He lights a cigarette, takes a long drag, and frowns. He begins, "We won't keep you long. There's really not very much to say, and we know you're on call today."

He looks around at the others and asks if any of them wants to say anything before he goes on. There is no response. Dr. Schwartz crosses his legs and tilts his head to the other side. Dr. Dunbar is staring into the middle distance. Dr. Faulkner glances impatiently at Dr. White and then looks back down at a paper on his desk.

My thoughts pass over the events and patient interactions of the past several months, and I am unable to come up with anything over which they may have taken serious issue.

Dr. White stares fixedly at me over his glasses and finally continues, "Well, we've gathered all the reports from your supervisors and reviewed them carefully, and of course some of us have had more personal contact with you than others, and the fact is . . ."

He breaks into a mischievous smile, "We all love you and think you're doing a fine job. Keep up the good work. That's really all, unless you have something you want to ask us?"

When I decline, he adds, "Oh . . . try to be on time a little more often?"

We all laugh and shake hands and I am almost at the door when Dr. Dunbar says, "Oh, Judy. There *is* just one thing. I spoke with Miss Finch, the nursing supervisor, the other day, and she was rather troubled, you might say."

He fingers his watch chain. "She said she's been trying very hard to get her nurses to dress more appropriately and is actually considering the possibility of putting them back in uniform if they don't make more of an effort at it. One of her major complaints was, however, 'How can I get my nurses to look decent when some of your female residents are walking around in jeans half the time?' Since you're the only woman doctor at the moment who has any contact with the inpatient wards, I assume she was referring to you."

I swallow my anger and say noncommittally, "Yes?"

"Well, we like to keep things as workable as we can in this department, and I think perhaps Miss Finch may have a point after all. Do you?"

"No, not really, Dr. Dunbar. If you'll forgive me for saying so, it sounds like the stuff I used to hear in high school—"

"I don't know what you mean by that."

"Well, you know, sort of rigid and authoritarian—"

Before Dr. Dunbar can reply, Dr. Schwartz steps in to mediate: "Look, Judy. As far as we're concerned, you can dress any way you please. But in this, as in any other business, unfortunately, there are always several sides to every question. And in this, as in any other business, one of the most important factors to consider if the place is to function effectively is—if Dr. Faulkner will excuse my making an unintentional pun—communication. If that breaks down, things fall apart rapidly. In this case, it's our communication with nursing that's at stake—"

"I understand what you're saying, Dr. Schwartz, but communication is one thing, surrender's another. And though I wouldn't want to make a big thing of it, I don't think the issue of dress is entirely irrelevant to the therapy I'm doing, especially when a number of my patients are in their teens and early twenties. Often we both feel more at ease in casual attire and that can sometimes break some of the ice and be therapeutically helpful."

"I think I probably agree with you to a point. I feel that the therapist, at least, should be comfortable with his or her own particular style, whatever that may be. But . . ."

He looks over at Dr. Dunbar, who has been scribbling something rapidly in a notebook and abruptly snaps it closed, clearly signaling something ominous and that he has nothing further to say about the matter for the moment.

Dr. Schwartz continues, "Well, let me put it this way. Use your own judgment about it. You know from working here that we're flexible and open and do our best to encourage people to reach their own potential their own way, and that we try to help when we can. Just know that we have our problems, too, and if you can think of any way to help us, we'd appreciate it."

"I'll certainly think about it, Dr. Schwartz. Maybe if I talked with Miss Finch myself and tried to explain—"

Dr. White blanches and stands up as he interrupts me, "For God's sake, don't do that!"

A little surprised at himself, he laughs nervously and says, "Look, I'm sure we're making a mountain out of a molehill and that this whole thing will just fizzle out in a week or so. Don't worry about it. Let us handle it. Here, let me get the door for you."

On my way out, I glance quickly over at Dr. Faulkner, who hasn't said a word. He smiles and winks, and I offer a silent prayer of thanks that there's a mad genius at the head of the department. His presence and intelligence somehow mysteriously enable the most diametrically opposed kinds of people to work and live together forty hours a week.

Before I can sort out my feelings further, my beeper summons me back to the emergency room.

The e.r. is now in full swing, with people in various stages of undress and need in the nine or ten different cubicles. Each cubicle is a complete unit, with a utility cabinet, a stretcher, a metal chair, a sink, and a wall attachment for a portable oxygen tank.

The emergency room of my medical school days was laid out in much the same way, but of course was more impoverished.

There were five cubicles, incompletely partitioned from one another by thin wooden dividers, so that the conversation and other sounds from one could easily be heard in the others. This was not entirely a disadvantage—if an emergent situation unexpectedly arose in an unattended cubicle, it was immediately broadcast to the entire staff in the large room.

My first night on duty as a medical student had been an unusually warm Dublin night, and the door to the Casualty Dept., as it is called there, had been left open to allow the fragrant sea-and-heather-heavy air to drift in and dilute some of the nasty antiseptic odor that hung about in the corners, on the floors and tables and sills. I had already overcome my opening-night stage fright by stitching up a workman who had cut his forearm on a piece of scrap metal, and we had both survived the suturing without losing consciousness. He had left smiling and grateful. Then I had sat down to bask in the pleasant glow of having done something concrete for someone for the first time in my early career, and only then, ten minutes after he had left, did my hands begin to shake.

I picked up the man's chart to write up my notes, when I heard a doggy sound at my feet and felt a cold, wet nose against my leg. It was one of those beasts whose only visible part in fact is a nose through all the hair. A gray-white stubble tail was wagging furiously. Then there was a little bark, and Alehouse, as I later learned the dog was called, wheeled around to escort an old man with a cane into the room. An area above the man's left eye was swollen and dark, and from the corner of the wound, an angry split that would require stitching oozed blood.

"How do you do, sir," I said. "Of the two of you, I assume you're the patient?"

"You're not Irish!" he snapped.

"That's right. I'm American. But I work here and even if I'm not from your country, I think I can do a pretty good job on your eye. Would you let me try?"

Despite his age, he took me in with a look of penetrating appraisal and native intelligence that would have equaled many a younger man. Apparently, he found nothing objectionable, for he and Alehouse sat down in one of the cubicles. The others were empty for the moment. The resident on duty came back from his coffee break, checked the injury, and felt I could handle it easily. I went in to take a history.

"May I have your name, sir?"

"Sean Kilmartin. And who might you be, if you don't mind my askin'?"

I told him my name and that I was a senior medical student at the hospital.

"Pleased to meet you, I'm sure." He stood up again and shook my hand. "And this is Alehouse, me closest friend and livin' companion." Alehouse and I also shook hands.

"How old are you, Mr. Kilmartin?" I asked, pen in hand, ready to record the information in the proper place. I looked up at his silence.

He winked and said, "Sure, you don't really need to know that now, do you? Well, let's say close on to ninety. I'm not really sure meself, you know. I was born at home in the country, you see, and me ma never had it written down exactly."

I wrote down ninety on the chart and took his address and other essential preliminary information.

"Now, Mr. Kilmartin, would you like to tell me what happened to your eye?"

His bushy white brows knitted fiercely together as the details of the event came back to him, and he began his account.

"Well, it started off ordinary enough, like any other night, you might say. Alehouse and I was down to the corner pub, The Stag's Tail, d'ye know it?"

I nodded.

"Well, I ordered me usual jar of stout and was sittin' talkin' to Declan Murray about the Baldoyle races today. I don't suppose you'd know anything about horses, would'ya?"

I ventured humbly, "A little."

"Well, anyway, we were wonderin' about Son of Kildare's chances for the Sweeps. You know, that kind of talk, like, when this young upstart comes in and starts arguin', would you believe. It started off with Son of Kildare and ended up with politics. Now *mind you, I believe in 'live and let live' and all that, but when it comes to Eamon de Valera, I'll hear no evil words said. So this young upstart says—"*

His wound was continuing to swell, and I realized that if I didn't get the cut sutured quickly, it was going to be almost impossible to do a neat job.

"Mr. Kilmartin, I don't mean to be rude, but your injury needs attention. Could you get to the point and tell me how you were wounded and whether or not you lost consciousness?"

"Well, of course I didn't lose consciousness! I never blacked out in me whole life! I'm fit as a trout!—if you don't mind me tellin' you, miss. Anyway, the talk got a bit heated, as I was sayin', and well, he clobbered me, he did!"

I was shocked to hear that a young man, especially in this rather gentle country, could get angry enough to attack a brittle old-timer physically.

"What did he hit you with, Mr. Kilmartin?"

"I don't know, I wasn't lookin'. His fist, I suppose."

After a final pat on Alehouse's head, I started to wash up for the procedure. Nurse Falkin wheeled in the sterile suture kit and antiseptics for cleansing the wound. Sean Kilmartin was a stoic. Through the entire operation, from the probing of the wound for foreign material, to the cleansing and debridement of the area, to the injection of the local anesthetic and the final stitching itself, there was not a sound, except for an occasional whimper from Alehouse.

Just as I was applying the penicillin gauze and protective bandages, we heard a crash, followed by loud, drunken swearing, and a subsequent general commotion. Alehouse left to investigate. A man was apparently ushered into another cubicle, and I heard Dr. Brown telling him to calm down and take the bloody bandage off his hand so he could see what was underneath.

"That's a nasty-looking cut, sir. It will need a lot of stitches," I could hear the resident saying. "How did it happen?"

The drunken reply was slow in coming, "Some old geezer hit me with his cane in a pub. We was—"

There was a sudden profane exclamation, which I gathered was prompted by the appearance of Alehouse in the man's cubicle.

"That's him! That's the old bastard's dog! Where is he?! I'll show him a thing or two, I will!"

Mr. Kilmartin, of course, had jumped up in response to all this, and tore open the curtain of his booth. We were confronted with the "young upstart," who couldn't have been a day under seventy-five at the least, fists clenched and at the ready.

There was a long, tense silence, during which the two old men stared murderously at each other. Then, almost simultaneously, the man noticed Mr. Kilmartin's bandage, and Mr. Kilmartin saw the other's badly bloodied hand. Tentatively at first, and then with unrestrained hilarity, Mr. Kilmartin threw back his head and laughed. After a moment of hesitation, the other man began to laugh as well. In a few minutes, the two were hysterical with tears of mirth rolling down their cheeks, and Alehouse barking in confused sympathy. Half an hour later, the three were out the door, planning to share a taxi home. I calculated roughly that their combined ages, including Alehouse, totaled around one hundred and seventy.

A powerfully built black man wearing an expensive ankle-length leather coat and mirror sunglasses leans out of Room 152 and brings me back to the present.

"Hey, nurse," he calls angrily down the corridor, "What's happenin' around here? I been waitin' almost an hour already, and this dude's in pain, man!"

One of the nurses goes in to talk to him, and as I continue toward my office, I hear him threaten, "Listen, baby, if you don't get a doctor in here fast, I'm gonna tear this place apart, you hear?"

Ah, for a little Irish humor in New York. Maybe in Ireland, too, these days.

There are again policemen, this time five or six of them, outside the room with my next patient. My heart sinks, and I think to myself, "God, it's going to be one of those days. Harry's nose was right."

Not even two o'clock and another one brought in by the police. Since the beginning of my residency, I have come to recognize a phenomenon of "bunches." Bunches of alcoholics, bunches of depressed, suicidal people, bunches of down-and-outers looking for a place to stay and mimicking "mental illness" to try and gain access to a bed and food, sometimes bunches of hours with nothing to do at all. One thing has become clear about the bunches of people I'll be seeing before nine o'clock tomorrow morning. Though there will be exceptions, a number of those I will meet in the hours to come will be psychotic and probably violent.

One look past the wall of police tells me that this patient is no Hettie Small. Tied face-down to a stretcher with about four sheets across various parts of his body, and hand-cuffed, is a handsome young man in his early twenties who looks a bit like a blond pirate. Masses of thick, weather-bleached curls cascading around his face and neck; a full, rich, mud-streaked beard; a black patch over one eye and an old jagged scar on his cheek; an open-necked Indian shirt; tight, well-worn, fading jeans, and leather sandals. Despite, or maybe because of, his excessive restraints, he is quiet just now, gazing somewhere into a world of his own.

One of the policemen describes how they were summoned to a local YMCA, where Sanford Hamilton III was standing on an overturned trash can preaching religion and sex to the people passing in and out of the lobby. When the police cars pulled up outside, Mr. Hamilton had jumped down from his dais and begun to tear up the room. He split a couch almost in half, broke several chairs, and knocked a man to the floor. It took six officers to subdue him, and by the time they succeeded, the lobby was a shambles.

I start into the room and a policeman says, "Watch out, doctor. Don't be fooled by all those restraints. He just bit one of my partners. He's up front being treated by one of your medical friends."

Mr. Hamilton watches me pull up a chair close enough to talk comfortably, but out of teeth range. The eye without the patch takes me in fully, almost instantaneously, and partly on that basis, I make an educated guess that the somewhat dilated pupil is probably not due to drugs but to the effects of an agitated psychosis. He has not moved or changed expression since my entrance, just quietly noted my every gesture and mannerism. I try to imagine what I would be feeling if our positions were reversed, and the closest analogy I can come up with is the primitive, desperate fear and rage an animal must feel when it is trapped and fighting for survival. Doubting that any amount of gentleness, sincerity, or reassurance can make any difference at this point in time, I nonetheless try as softly as I can, "Hello."

Still watching me closely and without much change in expression, he answers not entirely hostilely, "Hello yourself."

I turn my head and look at the police standing just outside the door, glance painfully over the handcuffs and restraints, then back at the vigilant blue eye and say, "I'm sorry about all this."

"You're okay. At least, you'll do," he pronounces definitively. "I might just decide to save you, woman."

"From what?"

Across the man's face a slow smile spreads and transforms itself into a hysterical leer, and then he begins to laugh. The laughter is loud, uncontrolled, at times piercing and wild. The police are getting edgy, but he makes no effort to resist the restraints. The episode continues for several minutes and eventually trails off into an occasional high-pitched, childlike giggle. He has either forgotten my question or chosen not to answer it. When he finally looks back at me, the expression on his face has become unmistakably malevolent.

"Who are you anyway?" he demands.

"I'm Judith Benetar, a doctor here. A psychiatrist."

His response is an inner explosion that I can feel before

anything actually happens. And what happens is fast and total. From deep in the man's throat comes a sound that I can only describe as a dangerous growl, and his lips curl back from his teeth in a vicious snarl. At the same time, all the muscles in his body have tightened and swelled, and the stretcher begins to creak under the strain. One of the sheets gives way, and the others show signs of weakening. For a second, I think that he cannot possibly sustain this super-human effort for more than a few seconds, but one look at his face warns me that I am mistaken.

I have to move fast. I call the police into the room to hold him down and shout for a nurse. Sue appears at the other end of the corridor, and I yell, "Fifty milligrams of i.m. Thorazine, fast!"

In less than a minute, Sue reappears and runs into the room with the injection, which she administers quickly and expertly. The man hasn't seemed to notice.

For all her years of nursing experience, Sue pauses at the door, startled, before returning to her other nursing duties. The Herculean effort is continuing against handcuffs, restraints, and five police officers. Veins in the patient's head and neck are bulging and purple. I begin to worry that the man will injure or possibly even kill himself in some way if this doesn't stop soon.

I go as close to him as I dare and say desperately, "Sanford, stop it, will you! You're scaring the shit out of us!"

Whether it's the statement or the Thorazine beginning to work, or maybe a little of each, there is a slight relaxation of muscle tension. The growling, at least, stops, and he says, "I am?"

"Yes, of course you are! Look around you."

The struggle ends. There is a brief pause, and then a kind of laughter begins again, shrill, somewhat whinnying, and in its way almost as frightening as the physical effort. When the full force of the Thorazine finally takes effect, the shrieking finally trails off, and Sanford Hamilton III, who-

ever he may be, bound, manacled, and drugged, lies pant-
ing and gasping for air.

Hoping for once that someone is abusing drugs, which
might be weaned from his system, I ask him quietly if he
takes anything.

"Only what you fucks stick into me every once in a
while. Nothing else—drugs are poison."

I try to get more information, but he turns his head away
and refuses to say any more. I leave a policeman on guard
and go into my office to arrange for a transfer to Bellevue.
One of West End General's biggest failings is that it has no
facilities for dangerously violent people, apart from the
"quiet room" on each floor, which is usually a very tempo-
rary measure in acute emergencies.

I take out the transfer form and fill in the necessary
details. In the space marked *Diagnosis*, I write, "Schizophre-
nia, hebephrenic type." Then I put my pen down, trying
to ignore the feeling of inadequacy and helplessness that
has gradually overtaken me. The final touch is always this
labeling, which says everything and nothing. A kind of
code by which we doctors try to communicate something
to one another, and also a way of trying to contain things
about which we have very little understanding. Give a
thing or a person a label and you have at least an illusion
of comprehension and familiarity, control maybe.

I leave some final orders with the nurses about medication and plead with Harry to try to hurry up the city
ambulance drivers so that Sanford won't have to remain in
such physical discomfort any longer than is necessary.
Some days it's taken six hours to get a patient transferred.
Harry says with a sigh that he'll do his best, but that he
can't promise miracles and you can't fight city hall—"Or
haven't you learned that yet, Dr. Benetar?"

"I don't know, Harry. I guess I change from day to day
about it."

"Then maybe you still have some 'growing up' to do, if

you'll forgive me for being so presumptuous."

"Could be, Harry. Hey, who's the shrink around here today, anyway?"

Harry looks around with exaggerated perplexity and says, "I don't know. Beats me."

"Gee, then maybe you'd better take over for a while."

"No way, Dr. Benetar! NO WAY! You couldn't pay me a million dollars to do the kind of work you people do. Thanks a lot, but I'll stick to my typewriter and frustrations."

He looks up at my face and suddenly becomes serious.

"Hey, you look beat. Why don't you go and get some coffee or something. It's only three thirty—you've still got about eighteen hours to go. Don't worry, I'll goose the ambulance drivers the best I can."

I thank him for his concern and say that maybe coffee's not a bad idea. As I walk away, I realize that taking a break now will mean missing a scheduled conference, but it might be well worth it. I check Sanford's room a last time, find his one eye closed, his breathing even and regular. The police ask my opinion about transfer, and I suggest that two of them, plus medication, should be adequate for management in the ambulance. I leave them discussing which two, and head for the cafeteria, thinking about Hettie, Victor, and Sanford, on some level hoping for them, on another feeling that all three have pretty well determined, established, and sealed their own fates in their own ways, leaving little opening or motivation for dialogue with another person who might be able to help them change their frames of reference. Even in the short space of time I have been practicing psychiatry, I have learned to recognize what I can only describe as a "burned-out" feeling from many of the people with whom I come in contact, as in my medical days, I was often able to detect a certain cancerous look in patients before a malignancy had been definitively diagnosed.

On the other hand, it is sometimes hard to contain my exuberance when I detect a real reaching-out, a readiness for communication, room for movement and growth.

I pull open the large door to the cafeteria. The huge room is almost deserted. The cashier dozes over her register. An exhausted-looking obstetrician in his fifties hunches indifferently around a cup of coffee, white coat spattered with dried blood, heavy pouches under his eyes and at least twenty-four hours of growth on his chin. Two lab technicians in a far corner argue in muffled tones. The rest of the hundred-odd tables are empty, and the place looks functional and unwelcoming, reminding you, in case you might just happen to forget for a moment, that THIS IS AN INSTITUTION—ADJUST YOUR HEAD TO THE PROPER MENTAL SET. But somehow I am caught, and even a walk across the street to the Greek luncheonette suddenly seems too great an effort. Fatigue and inertia propel me toward the aluminum coffee urn.

I wince at the mountain of styrofoam cups next to it. The regular cups and saucers are stacked neatly in wire baskets just out of reach. Strangely, it annoys me enough to call an attendant and ask her for one of each. She gives me a nasty glance and is about to make some remark, but apparently decides it isn't worth it and merely clatters a cup and saucer across the counter at me and walks away without a word. A moment of quiet despair is saved by the realization that the obstetrician must have done the same, and I glance with a rush of warmth at his slouched back.

I take a table not far from him, facing a window. The clouds and rain are so heavy and dark that it has already begun to look like evening. I shudder involuntarily despite the heat in the room. Relentless days and nights of this in Dublin, with no relief from the damp and cold, not even indoors.

Our first year in medical school, I hardly ever remember being out of my fur-lined coat. The cuffs were discolored for several inches from the formaldehyde of the dissecting room. Ben and I together with numb fingers and scalpels because they thought a husband and wife might like to work as a team. On a cadaver? Ah well, I suppose they were only trying to do "the right thing" by us. Starting with the thorax and upper limb, we carefully began to peel away the skin of a dead man. Ben furious with me because I couldn't eat meat for a month.

"It's absurd, Judy! What the fuck does one thing have to do with the other?"

"I don't know, Ben! Everything. . . . I'm sorry, but your roast beef looks like the chest muscles on our cadaver. I'm sorry, okay? I can't help it."

"Oh, Christ, you're impossible!" He had thrown his fork on the plate, splashing gravy across the table.

"What kind of friggin' doctor are you gonna be if you can't even be clinical about some stupid corpse that's been dead for months?"

"Leave me alone! I'll get over it. Just leave me alone."

"God, you're so touchy and sensitive, I can't say anything to you anymore."

That was maybe the beginning of a clear lack of communication that was later to become more serious and final. Not long afterward, Susan and I were scrubbing up in the women's washroom after an anatomy lab. Unexpectedly, this stoic daughter of English aristocracy threw her nail brush in the sink, muttered an unmistakable "Damn!" under her breath, and disappeared into the next room. I found her crying on a bench cluttered with soiled lab coats. When I asked what was wrong, she mumbled, "Nothing. . . . It's just the smell of formaldehyde; it won't come off!" and buried her face in her coat. I put my arm around her shoulders and felt her tremble and heave with emotion.

She looked up with an angry vehemence and said, "Judy, do you realize we'll never be the same? That we've voluntarily committed ourselves to a profession that will separate us from other people? That things like terminal illness and death will become common-

place to us? It's hateful, simply hateful! Who do we think we are anyway?" WHO DO WE THINK WE ARE ANYWAY? *A question that follows me around daily.*

In the half hour of talk that followed, we may have found more consolation than Ben and I had given each other in weeks. And it was Susan who saw me blanch and guided me quietly out of the anatomy lab the day the hand hit me in the face.

I had been holding the arm of our cadaver out away from the torso, so that Ben could be freer to work in the armpit. I was getting tired and about to suggest that we change places, when Ben's scalpel severed a muscle, and the arm suddenly rotated ninety degrees at the elbow, as if it had a life of its own. The hand, with its curled fingers and long, yellow nails, came up and bit me unexpectedly, scattering formalin and bits of dissected flesh and fat in my face and hair. I dropped the arm and Ben said, "Shit, Judy! You nearly made me cut the brachial artery!"

I think I remember Susan saying calmly, "Work on something else for a while, Ben. We'll meet you at Donnelly's for coffee in an hour."

She guided me, unseeing, upstairs, and it was my turn to break down. Susan turned on a small electric heater in the damp gloom of the washroom and listened to me tell her it was only the hand that really bothered me, that I had really become objective about the rest of it, but that somehow the hand seemed more real, more connected with life. She waited and said nothing, and eventually I got down to it, bewailing my vulnerability, sobbing that Ben was right, I would never make a good clinician because I couldn't seem to be clinical about anything and maybe I should just give it up now and call it a day. Hysterical women had no place in medicine. At the time, it did not occur to me that culturally and historically, men do different things with their distress. Like act it out in various socially acceptable ways, or bury it and have their heart attacks in their forties and fifties.

Susan was supportive and reassuring, the moment passed, and so in time did most of my qualms. Our cadaver, whom Ben had nicknamed "Butch," in lieu of the Number 23 on a card tied to his toe, began to have less resemblance to anything I could call human as we dissected more and more of him and as he started to dry out over the months, in spite of our formalin-soaked wrappings.

I remember only one other rough moment in anatomy. When we reached the genitalia, I refused point-blank to have any part of the dissection of Butch's testicles and penis, nor would I participate in the proceedings on the neighboring group's "Maggie." I made it a point to learn the details from Gray's Anatomy *and plaster-of-paris models but stayed away from the lab for three days.*

When I returned, it was obvious that others had had some difficulty with the region also. Ben, who was a meticulously careful and skilled dissector, had rendered Butch's masculinity unrecognizable; Maggie had been macerated, and offhand, I can't remember a well-dissected specimen in the room. Uncharacteristically, Ben admitted with some embarrassment in an unguarded moment that it had been "too much, Judy. Every time I made an incision, I felt it in my balls."

Shivering in the chilly gloom of the lecture theater, listening to his account, watching his tired, serious gray eyes grow tense with worry about the weekly "spot" exam on Saturday morning, I wondered what in hell we were sacrificing our souls to. Six months before, we had been lying on a beach in Crete wondering about Greek gods and olives. I touched my husband's arm, and he looked up and understood for once.

"It's okay, kid. We'll be all right, you'll see," he said softly.

He put his arm around me and drew me closer on the ancient wooden bench. "Poor Judy. When the hell are you gonna stop shivering? Christ, the dampness never lets up in this frozen greenhouse of a country—can't even sit and take a crap in comfort. And do you know how long it's been since I've seen your body, woman? Why don't we starve for a while and buy some kind of efficient heater for that iceberg of a flat?"

I nestled into his neck and murmured something about going home to bed and missing the lecture. Our English and Irish classmates began to straggle in and laughed at the picture of us huddled in the huge amphitheater in our overcoats under a bust of Sir John

Cunningham. Rosy-cheeked and buoyant, they made gentle fun of our American metabolism and dependence on central heating. Someone passed around a flask, and Sean Murray asked a question about the cutaneous nerves of the thigh.

Ben pulled out a piece of paper and began to illustrate the answer. Without looking up, he said, "Later, Judy, okay?" and went on with his explanation. The moment was gone. There were not many others to follow.

The sound of a chair being pushed away from a table brings the room back into focus. I look around to see the obstetrician standing in his creased green operating-room trousers, drawstring knotted at the waist, taking a last drag on his cigarette. He stubs out the butt, catches my eye, and throws me a weary smile, then lumbers away to the conveyor belt, rattling stained cup and saucer in one hand. As he leaves the cafeteria, he absentmindedly pulls off the green cloth cap he has probably been wearing for hours. It has left an odd line across his forehead, and his thick gray hair is matted and clumped. The door creaks faintly at his exit, and then the room is suddenly very empty.

"Miss, we close in five minutes until suppertime." The cashier points to her watch and I suppress a petty annoyance. This woman has seen me almost daily for nearly a year, sometimes stethoscope in hand, and it has not once occurred to her that I might be a doctor at this hospital.

I nod and swallow the rest of my coffee. On the way out, something impulsive stops me by the wall telephone, and I call Alan and ask if he'll cover an extra hour for me, so that I can walk to my shrink's.

"In this weather? What are you, crazy or something?"

"Yeah. That's why I'm going to my shrink."

"Ach, so—I zee—very interestink! Yeah, sure, Judy. I'm not especially busy now. Two of my patients canceled this afternoon."

"Thanks, Alan. You're a sweetheart."

"Ain't it the truth, though. Don't get too wet out there."

A little after four o'clock. The streets like a picture through a blue-gray filter. Brilliant red light glowing through the haze stopping traffic. Rain transformed to a fine, penetrating mist which settles instantly in a film on my face and on my weathered trench coat. Pointless to open the umbrella. I put up the collar of the coat, fasten the top button under my neck, and begin to walk east.

Apart from its immeasureable personal value, my therapy has been perhaps the most significant tool of learning in dealing with patients since I began my psychiatric residency. Though it is not a requirement for training, it is highly recommended, and with time I have come to appreciate the rationale more fully. Unless a therapist is aware of his or her own hangups and how they affect relationships with other people in general, at some perhaps critical point in their interactions with a patient, they may intrude on the therapeutic process.

It is also invaluable in learning to work as a psychiatrist to have the experience of *being a patient.* There is a strong, subtle, qualitative difference that cannot be really understood unless it is lived. To be identified as the one who has problems (and strengths) to define, articulate, and work on; to trust another human being enough to share one's absurdities and personal distortions; to experience the inadequacies and failings of the doctor-patient relationship from a patient's point of view; to feel the discoveries that one has made in one's head begin to influence the "gut" ways of functioning; to begin to appreciate a certain sense of inner freedom that comes with discarding antique inhibitions and fears; to contemplate from an intimate perspective areas of common ground with others, and to feel validated as a person, is a lesson in humanity and compassion that may well be essential to the effective care of another person.

On a corner near my psychiatrist's office, a gigantic, steam-driven pile driver attacks the rubble and stone through a window in the makeshift wall of old doors, spewing enormous clouds of white vapor from its mechanical belly. A notice describes the thirty-two-story apartment building going up on the site. It is the third in the neighborhood in a year.

When I began treatment with Mel Bernstein, they had been knocking down a building on his block. A sign in the abandoned luncheonette on the street level had advertised two eggs, coffee, and toast for breakfast for 53 cents. For some reason, it had made me uncomfortable to see the crumbling bricks and stone, and I would walk past with face averted. My marriage was also crumbling then, and on some unconscious level, the analogy was too painfully concrete.

As I cross the street to Mel's entrance, I glance absently in the window of the expensive boutique that has replaced the luncheonette. The office door is open, and Mel beckons me in.

The room has the embrace of a warm and unusual intelligence. Papers and journals scattered haphazardly across the top of the ancient, battered desk. Books stuffed at odd angles in between the laden shelves that extend floor to ceiling on two of the office walls. Gifts from friends and patients lodged in incongruous resting places—the statue of a woman bent and weeping; a bronze horse in flight; the multicolored, mosaic face of a happy, puzzled child; a pen-and-ink sketch of the country in winter; a laughing, golden lion against a background of royal-blue sky and stars. On the table near my reclining leather chair, a bunch of ferns and daisies, and a box of animal crackers left by some youthful predecessor.

The deep-set, knowing dark eyes watch me with care and thoroughness and a gentle acceptance. They wait.

"I'm on call today. It's awful. It always takes so much out of me. . . . I feel so helpless most of the time, so vulnerable. Do you know what I mean?"

He nods and says, "Yes, I know," and resumes the silent, careful watchfulness.

I grow vaguely uneasy and begin to study my necklace. Then, in a feeble attempt to relieve the tension, I try thoughtfully, "Sometimes I'm not sure if you represent my mother or father or stepfather. It may change at different times, I guess. But if you're my mother, then—"

He cuts me off abruptly. "If you don't mind, Judy, could we dispense with bullshit psychiatric intellectualizations? Why don't you try grappling with some of that anxiety instead?"

"How, Mel? My mind's a blank."

He fingers a reprint in his lap and says casually, "Why don't you start by just telling me how you feel now?"

He puts the paper on the coffee table to my left and waits. I cannot read the title upside down. I look away and wish I were somewhere else.

"I wish I were somewhere else. . . . I don't want to be here today."

"How come?"

"Dunno." My hands are wet and clammy. "Scared, I guess. I had a dream last night I don't really understand and I'm somehow embarrassed to talk about it. . . ."

"After all this time in therapy, Judy? Must have been a heavy dream."

"Yeah, I guess so. It's funny, you know? Dreams don't usually give me so much trouble. I even wrote this one down and then forgot to bring the paper in with me to work this morning—and I spent an hour last night writing the damn thing down."

"Yes, and if you keep telling me how much trouble you had with this dream, you'll use up another hour and avoid talking about it altogether."

My laugh sounds nervous and false. "Shit, I can't get away with anything in here, Mel."

I try to swallow and can't. To communicate an inner terror to another human being very often implies giving it up.

"Well," he says, "I'm not entirely sure what it is you'd be getting away with if it means hanging on to shadows and fears—"

"That's the kind of thing I'd say to *my* patients. God, life's full of mirror images and repetitions."

I pause a moment, intrigued with the thought and its implications. It is an effort to get back to the work and the system at hand.

"Anyway, it's easy to agree with you, Mel, but not so easy to feel. To answer your question, I think what I'd be getting away with by hanging on to shadows and fears would be a kind of self-definition, maybe a personal myth by which I live—one that's been around a long time and feels somehow comfortable by its familiarity. Does that make any sense at all?"

He half nods, not wanting to interrupt my flow of thought.

"I mean—how can I say it? It's not that I enjoy being afraid. It's that in some situations, I'm sort of used to responding with a particular kind of fear and confusion. And if I work it through, either with you or by myself, if I gain some understanding about what's going on in those situations and how I behave in them, then I'm faced with a totally new problem and somehow one that seems much scarier."

"And that is?"

"That is that the next time a similar situation comes up, I, with my new understanding of it, have to act differently. In essence, I guess what I'm saying in plain language is that I have to face the unknown head-on and not have a crutch to fall back on."

Mel Bernstein smiles. "Crutches are safe and known, even if they're old and obstructive and unnecessary, is that it?"

"Yes, I think so—and what would I do, where would I go, if I found I could walk without them? You know, ever since I started my residency in psychiatry, I've been repeatedly struck by the power of the status quo. This morning Elaine told me she actually enjoys acting like an infant. And think of the Jews in Germany just before the war, who sensed, maybe knew, what was coming and stayed anyway, hung on, if you will. Anything to avoid the unknown, even the threat of extermination."

"Okay, Ms. Sartre, now that we've defined the stakes, how about this dream you mentioned some time back?"

"I was on the eleventh or twelfth story of an old building. The framework was of wood, and the wood was rotten and cracked. It was dangerous to be there, and I thought about stopping the work I was doing and trying to get out before it was too late. I had been working on some files. My supervisor came along and asked me why I was staring out the window when there was so much work to do. I told her—"

"What did she look like?" Mel asks.

"Gray-haired, late fifties, uptight, but somehow enervated."

"Go on."

"I told her I was just about to take my lunch hour, which wasn't true, but I had to get out of the building before it crumbled. She said, 'Nonsense. Get back to the work I gave you.' I got very angry and said that I was entitled to a lunch hour. She said, 'As long as you work here, you'll do what I tell you.' I angrily threw a book on the floor and said, 'I quit!' "

"What kind of book, Judy, do you know?"

"Funny you should ask; yes, I do know. It was some kind of illustrated history book I had been reading when I should have been working. . . . Anyway, she said if I wanted to quit, that was fine with her. I was sort of disappointed that she didn't put up more of an argument after all the time I'd been working there, but turned on my heel and walked to the elevator. It was broken and I began to get scared about getting out of the building at all. I could hear my supervisor laughing. I said, 'You know, this building has been condemned by the Board of Health. It's going to fall down.' She walked away and said, 'Bullshit.'

"I couldn't get out by the stairway either. It was nailed shut with boards. I could feel the building sway and creak. Rats were dropping down through the holes in the ceiling, and I could hear beams and rafters giving way.

"I looked out the window and wondered if I would live if I jumped into the river below. A rat fell on my face and I did jump. The river was deep and I plunged way to the bottom. There was a lot of garbage and a sign stuck in the mud that said *Fight Pollution*. The water was thick and dirty. When I finally swam to the surface, I saw that my supervisor had sent a deputy to catch me. He jumped in the river and I began to swim to the opposite bank. I wasn't sure I could make it in time, since my clothes were wet and heavy, and the man was big and powerful and unencumbered."

"What do you mean, 'unencumbered'?"

"He was nude."

"All right."

"I made it just ahead of him. I climbed up on the bank gasping for breath, exhausted, but I was terrified that the man would catch me. I found a hammer lying in the grass and began to hit him with it before he could climb out of the water. His head got all bloody, and after I hit him several times, he stopped struggling to get at me. Eventually, his body was dragged away in the current. I didn't know if he was still alive.

"I felt dizzy and lay down on the bank to rest. I was

strangely exhilarated, but guilty that I had enjoyed my
savagery. I was also vaguely troubled that the deputy
would recover and come back for me. But mostly, I was
tired after the fight and thought I could always sort things
out after a short nap. I started to fall off to sleep and woke
up from the dream."

After a moment of thoughtful silence, Mel asks, "And
how did you feel when you woke up?"

"Confused about what it might all mean, but strangely
peaceful."

Mel starts to clean his glasses.

"So what do you make of it and what was your anxiety
and your reluctance to talk about it about?"

"I don't know—I guess the woman supervisor was pretty
obviously my mother. The hard part for me is the deputy.
Yes, I think that's what my anxiety's about. I guess I'm
afraid to admit that I think the deputy might have been
you. And that's really embarrassing, Mel, because I don't
think I see you as a deputy of my mother's in any sense of
the word. And the only other thing I can figure out is that
maybe the deputy was a part of my own head that tries to
keep me in a 'rotten place.' Which do you think, Mel?"

"Why not both?"

"Oh . . ."

"Well?"

"Yeah, maybe, but it's so unfair! You're not really like
that."

He smiles and the lines at the corners of his eyes wrinkle.
"Since when are we here to discuss what things are 'really
like,' hmmm? Isn't it the way you see them? And by the
way, my up-and-coming psychiatrist, in all your lectures
and readings, etcetera, did you ever happen to come across
the term 'transference'?"

"Yes, sure, but how . . . oh. You mean, if I've seen most
men in relation to my mother as submissive or 'deputies,'
why not you?"

"Something like that, yes. But the other part of what you said is also important—that it's really 'a part of your own head' that keeps you subservient, 'doing a job' you don't want in that 'rotten place.' By the way, how do you feel about killing the deputy off and quitting the job with the boss?"

"A little guilty."

"But not very, I think."

"No, not very."

We look at each other and laugh. The tension recedes among the comfortable, chaotic books.

Mel shifts in his chair and asks, "How are your mother and stepfather these days, anyway?"

"Pretty well. I just got a note from them, and they sound pretty good. Maybe that's why I had the dream. They're into all the usual craziness with each other, I'm sure. But somehow it doesn't seem as intense as it was. And neither of them has had a drink for months, in fact almost a year. Their letters, believe it or not, have actually been pleasant lately. Not one 'ungrateful, inconsiderate, thoughtless-and-cold daughter' line for ages. It's funny, but I don't feel nearly so angry with them as I used to."

"Well, if you see yourself as not 'working' for anyone else anymore, then maybe you have less to be angry about."

"You know, Mel, for all the drunkenness and the hobo-like existence we led when I was little, schlepping from place to place, living in tacky rented apartments in different parts of the country, watching them drink themselves into various hospitals and alcohol-rehab farms, and so on, I think that somehow, in between, they managed to be quite loving at times. And they really tried to give me things. I remember appreciating that about them, even when the gift backfired. Like the time they scraped some money together and sent me to a riding school and day camp in Florida. How could I tell them how miserable I was there when I knew how much it had cost them?"

"Why were you so miserable? I thought you loved horses and were quite a good rider."

"I was, I am. And I even won second prize in the horse show we had at the school at the end of the year—I might have won first prize if I'd had the 'proper dress.' We were really very poor in Florida, and when the bus came to pick me up every morning for this camp, I was the only kid who didn't have a riding habit. The other kids were from upper-middle-class or wealthy homes. I'd feel like a freak in my patchy jeans and T-shirt and saddle shoes. They mostly ignored me, except toward the end of the summer when I was doing so well in the riding classes. Then the indifference turned into open dislike and contempt.

"My parents came to the horse show and they were very proud when they pinned the red ribbon on my horse's bridle. My mother wore a shiny, synthetic-silk brown dress she had bought at Robert Hall's, and my stepfather had on a white shirt and his usual baggy trousers. Everyone else was dressed to the teeth, and the women wore jewelry that clanked and made some of the horses start when they patted their noses. We were a really curious trio in the middle of all that class."

Mel says, "I'm surprised they gave you a prize at all."

"So was I. And so was everyone else, I think. Whey they announced that first prize went to Sondra Mellingham, a pretty, petite, dark-haired girl with her hair braided up around her head under her riding hat, there was a loud round of applause, and a tall, blond woman dressed in white said, 'Oh, my baby! How wonderful!' Then they announced my prize, and there was a kind of curious silence. I guess nobody knew who I was. When the judges came over with the ribbon, my mother started to cry, and there were a few scattered handclaps. I was very proud, but also very embarrassed. I couldn't wait to get out of there with my ribbon. Later, for a treat, my parents took me to Howard Johnson's for dinner."

We sit in silence for a while and I become aware of the ticking of the clock. I look over to see how much time is left. We have about ten minutes.

"I've been thinking a lot about growing up lately and wondering why it all didn't overwhelm me. Apart from the fact that my parents were probably more loving than I usually give them credit for, another thing that I came up with is the realization that things were always either black or white—the choices were always pretty clear. It was always sort of a live-or-die climate. Do you know what I'm saying, Mel? For instance, some of my craziest patients come from nice, middle-class homes where the shades of gray are so subtle, you can't separate things out and maybe you flip out trying to."

"It's an interesting theory," Mel replies as he looks up at the bookshelves, "and some rather learned people have speculated about it. I can give you the references sometime. Of course, there are no sound conclusions. Not enough work has been done on the people who never show up in a psychiatrist's office or hospital, that is, the 'healthy people,' and what their life histories are like. And of course it's always difficult to make comparisons of that nature; there are so many variables and intangibles. I doubt if our kind of work can ever fit effectively into a scientific paradigm."

"Thank god."

"I agree," Mel says, "but a lot of people don't. Some of the more classical analysts, particularly. Anyway, it's a thing to think about. Your life history would cause a few psychiatrists, at least, to wonder how you survived."

"Funny. Dr. Nathan, the ward administrator on Castle ten, asked me that the other day."

"Sure. There are psychotic people walking around with seemingly far more benign pasts than yours. But as I said, we tend to forget the people we never see. There may be well-integrated, stable members of our society who've never thought to consult a psychiatrist and whose histories are horrendous."

"I know some doctors, including some of my supervisors, who might take issue with that statement."

"Undoubtedly. But then, it seems that you're part of the argument against them. Not that you don't have things to work out. But with a background of alcoholic parents, changing homes, poverty, and the added burden of being a woman in this society, one would not expect you, from their point of view, to be where you are."

"But I keep having this recurrent feeling of being an imposter. That one day I'll be found out and relegated back to that crumbling building in the dream, that I really belong there, or maybe that I never actually left it."

Mel looks at his watch.

"Well, I wouldn't know," he says flippantly. "Sometimes your image of yourself sounds like a bad Charlie Chaplin movie."

I glare at him, furious at his irreverence. He stares back, expressionless. Then something indefinable happens, and we both begin to laugh, softly at first, then with real hilarity. We share an ancient moment of wonder at the absurdity, the paradox, the tragicomedy of human existence.

"Well, anyway," he adds as he stands to open the door, "I guess part of you, at least, is ready to hit me or anyone else over the head who tries to stop you from crossing rivers!"

The apartment is dark on my return, smelling faintly of sweet wet earth from the tangled, lush garden that must be brought indoors from the oversize terrace one of these days. The cats stretch and yawn in the half-light from the hall. Clyde comes to greet me first, doing his alley-cat imitation of Mae West the length of the living room. Sam spends at least a minute untangling a Siamese claw from the mohair travel rug on which he has been sleeping, somehow trips and stumbles himself free, and finally gathers what is left of his dignity around him and makes his pigeon-toed, cross-eyed way down the hall to join us.

We share some herring from a jar in the refrigerator, and they sit down side by side, blinking up at me as I phone the hospital operator for messages. Clyde the bona fide street cat, crooked, misshapen, ridiculous, and brazen, curiously unkempt for a cat, is a born and sensitive actor with a special flare for mimicry and a repertoire that includes ostriches, dogs, sphinxes, and Mae West, his favorite. He is also self-appointed guardian to gentle, giant Sam, whose constant confusion and miscalculation render him somewhat vulnerable and accident-prone. I turn from them and stare out at the windows of the Dakota shining through the drizzle a few blocks away. The operator connects me with Alan, who tells me to take it easy for a while, the e.r. is quiet for the time being.

"The only thing you should know about, Judy, is that Grace Blackwell, that patient of Larry's, came in about an hour ago. He was right about her depression. I thought she was pretty suicidal and admitted her to Castle ten. Everything's done on her, though, orders, physical exam, medication, etcetera. Just wanted you to know she's there. I'll call Larry and tell him about her before I leave. I'll also tell the operator to call you at home if anyone wants you."

"Thanks, Alan."

"Right. How was your shrink appointment? Are you cured yet?"

"I'll let you in on a little secret. There was never anything wrong with me in the first place. I just go for the fun of it and to keep up appearances."

"Oh. You pay somebody forty dollars an hour for fun?"

"Sure."

"Ach, gott, she's a sick goil! You better get yourself to a good doctor. Listen, I hope you have a quiet night. I'll put up a sign on the front door telling them all to go to Bellevue. Take care. I gotta run."

"Okay. Thanks again."

The cats follow me into the bathroom. Two blossoms have come out on the African violet on the windowsill. When everything else is dying for the winter. As I undress for a shower, Clyde bats his Ping-Pong ball around the tub, making an incredible clatter, and I wonder aloud to him about how he managed to get it in there. He squawks and dashes out of the room in mock fear when I turn on the water, leaving the ball ricocheting around the tile. Sam looks on from the edge of the sink in cockeyed bewilderment, then curls up in the basin and rests his chin on the faucet waiting for me to bathe.

The water feels great, and I take a chance that I won't be called too soon and stick my head under the shower. My hair flattens out along my neck and back, just reaching the tip of my shoulder blades. The remembrance of my body is reassuring. I think back to the session with Mel Bernstein and realize that a good part of the reason for my survival has been an ability to stay in contact with, and to believe in, a certain animal instinct for self-preservation.

Running in fields with a half-breed Labrador retriever when things at home got too heavy. Angrily kicking up tufts of grass in an untended apple orchard and stopping breathlessly to gape when one of them uncovered a nest of baby rabbits. Climbing trees and one day discovering Mrs. Winlow from a branch behind her house.

"Won't you come in and have a cup of tea, dear?" She was a plump, gray-haired woman in an apron, hanging up clothes in her back yard. "You can bring your dog in, too. I might have a nice bone for him."

Walking into this perfectly ordinary-looking two-story white frame house on the edge of a small town in the Hudson River Valley, only three houses away from the one where we had rented a one-bedroom apartment six months before. While Mrs. Winlow busied herself with a kettle, she sent me in to the living room and told me to make myself at home. A little girl was asleep on the overstuffed sofa. There were two chickens dozing on the other end. An ancient bloodhound thumped a greeting with its tail. There was a noise on the staircase to my left, and I turned just in time to see a nanny goat and her kid disappear into one of the second-floor bedrooms. Cats were everywhere. My dog started barking excitedly, and I had to put him outside. Mrs. Winlow gave him a big soup bone, and he settled down with it in the grass. Then she introduced me to her daughter, who had been wakened by the racket. I realized there was something wrong with her from the empty stare in her eyes and the strange, thick tongue protruding from her mouth.

Mrs. Winlow said, "Rita, this is Judy. She lives nearby and may come to visit us sometimes."

Rita and I shook hands, and she said something like "Huni," because her mouth would not let her make the right sounds for my name. Then we sat down to tea and muffins, Mrs. Winlow and Rita on the sofa with the chickens, and I in a big, dusty armchair, somewhat apprehensive about squashing an egg or maybe a hidden kitten. From a kind of childish pride, I suppose, I put on my best manners and pretended that everything was perfectly normal and that I was used to this kind of thing. I fleetingly wondered if I might be dreaming or in some kind of play. I had just read Peter Pan the week before.

"Now then," said Mrs. Winlow, "tell us all about you," and smiled sweetly.

Later, Mr. Winlow came home from work. Mrs. Winlow had already told me that he worked for IBM. He was a small, wiry man with a twinkle in his eye, and he sized me up with a quick glance that was somehow altogether gentle and welcoming.

"I hope you don't mind our various house guests," he said. "My wife and Rita get a little lonely with me away at work all day and Paul off in the army."

He talked to me as though I were an adult, and I felt even better. I went back many times to visit and have tea before we moved to another state. Once Paul came home on leave, and I developed my first crush. He kissed me on the forehead before I went home, and

*I lay awake all night thinking about it. The next day, he was
already gone, when I got back from school.*

*The Winlows taught me something about love and coping. I
think we moved to Jersey in the fall.*

The phone rings through the water in my ears. I stumble
over Clyde dozing in the doorway and catch it on the
fourth ring.

"Hello?"

"Is this Dr. Benetar, then?" The lilting Irish voice
sounds very close.

"Yes, that's right." I try to sound calm.

"Just a minute, love. I've a call for you from Dublin.
Hold on now, please."

There is a moment of crackling and spitting, which I
presume has to do with thousands of miles of Atlantic cable
scraping along an ocean floor.

"Darling?"

"John! God, I thought you were the emergency room!"

"Well, I should hope not! Are you on call tonight? How
awful for you."

"How are you, John? You sound so British. . . . It's been
forever since I've heard your voice."

"British! That's heresy, woman! Just because I went to
school there and my middle name is Wellington. . . . Judith,
how are you?"

"Well, darling. Missing you terribly. And dripping! I
just got out of the shower."

"God, how wonderful! And I know—I miss you, too. In
fact, that's mainly what I phoned about. I can't bear it
much longer. I'm coming over for a while, if you'll have
me."

The news is totally unexpected, and I find myself staring
dumbly at the receiver while the cable crackles in my ear.

"Hello? Judith, are you there?"

"No. I just had a cardiac arrest. When are you coming?"

"Well, that's partly up to you, but if the first week in December would be all right—"

"Jesus, yes, please. The first week in December is lovely! That gives me enough time to ask for some days off."

"Can you, darling?"

"Yes, I think so. John, is there anything you'd like me to do in New York while you're here, anything I can plan for?"

"Yes. You can stock the refrigerator for a week and pull the phone off the wall. Think you can manage that?"

"Yes. Sounds marvelous."

"How are Sam and Clyde?"

"Ridiculous as ever."

"That's good. I'd hate to think they'd turned into normal cats all of a sudden. Say hello for me. By the way, we're going to be cut off anytime now, so if we're abruptly disconnected, don't be upset. And much as I love the image, please go and put some clothes on and keep yourself healthy for December, will you?"

"Okay. I love you."

"I know. It gets more and more intense. I—"

The lilting male voice returns.

"Time's up, I'm afraid. Sorry, love."

The line goes dead and then is replaced by a dial tone. The cats are sniffing the puddle at my feet. I hang up and throw the towel in the air.

"Sam! Clyde! John's coming! John's coming!"

They run in different directions and turn to look back at me incredulously. The next call summons me back to the hospital.

The police officer in the emergency room looks grave and troubled.

"I've never seen anything like this before, doctor. Apparently, the mother called up the psychiatrist on duty last night and said her daughter was acting 'a little strange.' The doctor advised her to bring the girl in for a consultation, and when she said she didn't think her daughter would come voluntarily, he suggested she get police assistance, especially if she thought the girl might harm herself or someone else. Well, the woman said no, it was nothing like that, just 'a little problem about eating.' And then I guess she hung up. It probably would have gone no further than this, but the hotel manager where they live threatened to evict them today if the mother didn't let the maid in to clean the daughter's room. He called us when the mother started giving him a hard time about it. Then my partner and I arrived and went up to the girl's room with the manager. It smelled like a zoo inside, and all the shades were pulled down. We turned on the lights and saw this skeleton girl lying in this crummy bed. She didn't look at us or say anything; she didn't even move or blink, but her eyes were open. And all the time, the mother's screaming at us that we had no right to go in there, her daughter had a college degree and had a right to her own privacy and who did we think we were barging in like that. She finally quieted down when my partner threatened to take her down to the precinct. Then we called the ambulance and brought them here. But I tell you, doc, I've never seen the likes of it. . . ."

Neither had I. We had been walking down the corridor from the front desk where the officer had been waiting for me, and as we pass through the swinging doors into the psychiatric area, I stop listening to his narrative. Sitting next to the policeman's partner is a middle-aged, obese woman with a pale, puffy face and very white, bleached blond hair. She clutches a black sequin bag in one hand and smokes nervously with the other. Beside her is a creature who resembles a photograph I once saw of a concentration-camp survivor, more dead than alive. She takes no apparent notice of our arrival. Her mother jumps up and says, "Are you here to see my Marybeth?"

"That's right. I'm Dr. Benetar. Would you both like to come into my office?"

Marybeth shows no sign of having heard. Her mother stamps out her cigarette and begins to light another.

"C'mon now, Beth," she says between her teeth, "you have to."

The girl stiffens almost imperceptibly.

I look over at Marybeth and say quietly, "No, you don't have to. Only if you want to. We can always talk here if you prefer, Beth."

Unexpectedly, the girl stands up. She sways noticeably, and the policeman steadies her. Her jeans, even belted, begin to slip down, and one bony, filthy hip protrudes, covered with nasty red swellings.

"On second thought, I think it might be better if we go into one of the other rooms where you can lie down, Beth, and the nurses can help you get cleaned up a bit before we talk."

The officers guide her, unresisting, into the nearest cubicle and help her onto a stretcher. I call one of the e.r. nurses and ask that Beth be bathed, at least preliminarily deloused, and medically checked out. The nurse stands for a moment in awed silence, then remembers herself and calls an aide for help in getting the girl undressed and into a hospital gown. I excuse myself and guide her mother into my office, wanting to get the interview with her over as quickly as possible.

"Doctor, you wouldn't believe this, but I swear to God it's true: My daughter got an M.A. in biology last year! She's not really like this. It's all just to spite me. *I'm* the one you should feel sorry for! Me, Janet Sloan!"

She points emphatically to her ample blue-taffeta chest, and as her voice gets louder, I realize that she has a speech defect that makes her sound as if she has a chronic heavy cold and swollen adenoids.

"Between her and that son-of-a-bitch who calls himself her father, I'll go crazy one of these days! And it's him you should blame for her being like this. He doesn't give a shit about her and never has. He—"

I interrupt and make an attempt to get some kind of coherent history from the woman. With difficulty, I am finally able to ascertain that Marybeth Sloan is twenty-seven, though she looks considerably younger, and she lives in an upper West Side hotel on a different floor from her mother, who shares her room with a man named Joe, whom she plans to marry in the near future, "if Beth don't screw things up, that is!"

Mrs. Sloan works as a file clerk and has spent most of her life in sleazy hotels, because she dislikes the responsibility of keeping a home. Beth's parents were divorced when Beth was two, and the girl grew up mostly with her mother, except for a year during her adolescence when Mrs. Sloan was being treated in a state mental hospital.

"You gotta understand, life was tough, bringing up a kid and all, and no support from anywhere. I just needed a little rest, that's all."

Beth's father is a wealthy textile manufacturer who supported his daughter financially during her childhood and later sent her through college, but saw little of her apart from occasional weekends and the year she spent with him during her mother's hospitalization.

"He treats her like dirt, that filthy bastard! He treats everybody like dirt. Spends all his free time with Playboy bunnies. Never thinks about anybody but himself!"

After being graduated from college, Beth had taken a cross-country trip with a few friends and then lived for a while in a commune in Haight-Ashbury.

"God knows what she did with those hippies! I kept telling her to drop those creeps and come back where she belonged."

Beth did, in fact, return to New York about a year ago, wiring her father for money for the trip. After starting and

quitting several part-time jobs, she had moved into her
mother's hotel, claiming she needed a rest. Mrs. Sloan was
not sure how long she had remained shut in her room or
when she had last eaten a meal.

"I gave up arguing with her weeks ago, after she attacked
me—*attacked* me, do you hear?"

"What happened, Mrs. Sloan?"

"Nothin'. I just told her she better damn well eat something and get her ass in gear or else I would come down and
sleep in her room and treat her like a baby, if that was the
way she was gonna act. Then I sat down on the edge of her
bed and told her to answer me or else—"

"Or else what?"

"I dunno. Nothin'. Anyway, that's when she hit me.
Right in the tit, too!"

She sits back and takes a long drag on her cigarette.

"What did you do then?"

"Just pushed her away and left the room and said, 'Okay
for you, if that's the way you want it.' She's always been
a scrawny brat, so I knew she wouldn't try anything else.
Anyway, I left her alone after that. She's always treated me
like a doormat, and I've just about had it with her. Like I
said, I'm sure this whole business is just to spite me. She's
a mean, spiteful girl, believe me. You'd never think to see
her as a kid that—"

The nurse interrupts and asks to speak to me privately.
I join her in the hall, where she is pulling off a pair of
surgical gloves.

"Dr. Benetar, we did our best, but that girl's a mess! Her
hair's all matted together and simply crawling! We Kwell-
shampooed it twice, but I think they may have to cut it off
after she's admitted. . . . You *are* admitting her?"

"Do you really have to ask?"

"Anyway, the other thing is that she's got a few bedsores.
I don't think she's moved or turned in weeks. Her backside
was covered with dried feces. I know it's hard to believe,
but apart from the bedsores and some signs of dehydration,

Dr. Cohen says she's medically clear. But he says to watch the bedsores; there are a couple of really bad areas over her sacrum."

She looks over her shoulder to make sure the door is closed. "I just don't understand it. How could anyone let her lie there all that time?"

I shudder and wonder aloud, "How can we do any of the things we do to each other in this world? By the way, did she say anything at all?"

"Nothing. And I forgot to tell you that she kept her arms in whatever position we put them in. I had to put her hands in her lap to keep her from holding them in the air. It was really freaky! Well, she's all yours now. . . . God, give me a bleeding ulcer any day!"

Back in my office, I tell Janet Sloan that I plan to admit her daughter to a psychiatric ward. She receives the information with a look of disgust, but surprisingly offers no protest.

"Well, you're the doctor," she says, grinding her cigarette out on the rug instead of in the ash tray beside her, "and I'm not gonna tell you your business. But remember, I brought this kid up. And there's nothing much wrong with her, in my opinion, that a good rap in the teeth wouldn't cure."

She opens the door and turns into the next cubicle, where her daughter is sitting with her hands in her lap as the nurse has left them. The skimpy white hospital gown hangs loosely on the skeletal frame, and a black laundry stamp with the words *Property of West End General Hospital* is visible just above her sunken chest. The nurse has left a turban-wrapped towel on her head. There is a strong smell of antiseptic.

Mrs. Sloan puts her hands on her hips and surveys her daughter critically. "So you finally made it. Congratulations! This doctor's gonna put you in the looney bin. I hope you're proud of yourself!"

The girl stares dully into some inner space. Mrs. Sloan

takes out another cigarette and then unexpectedly begins to cry. I hand her a tissue and she blows into it loudly.

"I don't know what I did to deserve this," she says, recovering enough to carefully wipe away some dripping mascara. With an ostentatious display of sudden affection, she pats Beth's hand and kisses her on the cheek, leaving a crimson imprint on the pallid skin. Then she draws herself up, embarrassed, and leaves the room.

She passes the police outside and says flatly, "Pigs!"

Janet Sloan pauses momentarily to light another cigarette, then struts provocatively down the hall, swinging her sequin bag.

"Beth, will you walk upstairs with me or shall I get a wheelchair for you?"

Nothing. I look around for a wheelchair and signal the policemen not to help. Still unresisting, she allows me to help her into it. The towel has loosened and fallen slightly to one side, and I find myself wondering absurdly if the weight of it will pull her over. At the foot of the elevator, one of the officers jots down my name, and they leave for their patrol car.

Angela Smith comes out of the nurses' station on Castle 12 and quickly conceals her shock.

"Hello, I'm Angela," she tells Beth warmly. "I'm one of the nurses here, and I guess we'll be seeing a lot of each other. I work here evenings from four to twelve. Right now, I'm going to take your temperature and blood pressure, okay?"

Angela and I simultaneously notice the louse making its way around the edge of the towel.

"Uh-oh," Angela quips, "I think I see an old friend from my schoolgirl days."

I call her aside and suggest another Kwell bath and shampoo. "And I guess we'd better put her in the quiet room until we get rid of the animal life."

"Right. Can I try giving her something to eat after that?"

"It's certainly worth a try, but I'm afraid I may have to

put down a feeding tube. Let me know if you have any success. I also want to examine her and talk with her when you're finished. . . . How are you, by the way? I haven't seen you for ages."

Angela grins broadly and the dark almond eyes glow in the smooth sienna skin.

"Great! My boy friend and I just got back from a vacation with my parents in Barbados. It was super!" As she turns to wheel Beth toward the bathroom, she adds, "It's good to be back, though, in a way. Couldn't tell you why, but I love this crummy city."

She pulls off a turquoise bracelet and puts it in the pocket of her cardigan, chatting to Beth about a nice hot bath and a glass of milk.

I sit down in the nurses' station to write an admission note and some routine orders on Marybeth Sloan, who has an M.A. in biology and a withdrawn catatonic psychosis.

Fortunately, I have been able to admit Beth to a floor that really practices the concept of the "therapeutic community." This is largely due to the efforts of Dr. Schuff, the ward administrator, who strongly believes in the value of a democratic community where all staff members and patients have an equal vote in community affairs and are encouraged to take responsibility for and to ventilate their feelings about the way the floor runs and might be improved. It is also often the community that resolves an issue for a troubled patient in ways that are not available to the patient's individual therapist.

Some of the other wards pay lip service to the idea of a therapeutic community, but often fail in significant ways for reasons that have to do with either a lack of real understanding of the concept, inferior personnel, or the vague fears of people in authority. The result is often a kind of puppetlike community atmosphere, which in fact is a hidden but felt authoritarian structure, frequently rigid and unreasonable in its dictates.

Even though Beth will be isolated in one of the "quiet"

rooms, so called because they are designed to minimize the amount of stimulation for violently out-of-control patients, she will be expected to participate in some ward activities almost immediately. When her lice have been eradicated and she is in better physical condition, she will be fully integrated into the program, which will include daily community meetings, communal meals, art and occupational therapy, patient planning meetings for outings and entertainment on the ward, group and individual therapy. Even if she is mute and minimally involved, her presence at these events is important. The impact of people on one another, in any situation, is immeasurably great, and it may, one hopes, be difficult for Beth to stay in the same remote, withdrawn place for any length of time.

Half an hour later, Angela accompanies me to the quiet room, where she has pillow-propped Beth on her side in bed to relieve pressure on the bedsores. It takes me a moment to realize what looks different about the girl. The thick, infested tangle of long black hair has been replaced by a short, wet shag-cut that exaggerates even more the sunken hollows of her cheeks.

"God, Angela."

"I had to do it," she whispers softly. Then louder, so that Beth will not be left out, "I explained to Beth that it was impossible to get the matted parts of her hair free with just shampoo, but since I used to work as a beautician for a while, I'd give her a sort of Jane Fonda cut, and if she didn't like it, she could always let it grow back in. I also told her a little bit about the way the ward functions and showed her around a bit. I said as soon as she's well enough, we'll move her into one of the two- or four-bedded rooms she just saw."

She slips the bracelet back on her wrist and turns to leave. "Well, if you don't need me for anything, I'll split for now. By the way, you were right. Beth doesn't seem to be too interested in food right now, at least not milk and

cookies. I left them on the bedside table, in case you want
to try again."

She closes the door silently, and I pull up a chair and sit
down facing Beth. The sight of the bony figure draped
shapelessly in institutional white, in a room stripped of all
but bare essentials, compels me to several long moments of
silence. I wonder briefly what to say to this woman in her
private void and know intuitively that a planned monologue will be meaningless. Sincerity, spontaneity, chance,
may count for something.

"Beth, I don't think I've really introduced myself to you.
I'm Judith Benetar. I'm a doctor, a psychiatrist, and my
work is to try to help people in trouble. I don't know yet
what your trouble is, but maybe between us we can find
out. Unless you have any objections, I'd like to be your
doctor."

I pause and consider the commitment I have just taken
on. Beth flickers her eyelashes but does not alter her blank
expression.

"I'll see you for an hour every day until you're better, so
we can get a sense of each other. I don't think I can listen
to myself talk for a whole hour every day though, so sometimes we may just sit in silence together, and sometimes,
perhaps, I could read to you. But I look forward to the time
when you will feel safe enough, or free enough, to say
something to me. Is there anything you might like to say
now?"

Another flicker of lashes and then nothing.

"I am first of all, before being a doctor, a human being
like yourself, and I have some firsthand experience of how
troubling and confusing life can be. Although it hasn't yet
overwhelmed me to the point where I've been unable or
unwilling to eat or talk, I can imagine that things must have
been pretty terrible for you to have drawn so far into yourself. In its own way, I suppose, it's a method of trying to
cope with danger or fear, and I guess one of the things we'll

have to talk about one day, when you're ready, is a different method of coping. One that works better for you, that allows you to stay in better touch with life and things of beauty. It can't be much fun to live in a prison of yourself."

Still expressionless, Beth moves her head slightly, and a few tears run across her nose and onto the pillow.

"I'm both sad and pleased to see you cry. It means that you haven't numbed yourself completely, that part of you *is* still in touch and can feel, even if it's pain." I wait, but nothing else is forthcoming.

"Until you're able to take care of yourself again, we'll take care of you. If you can't eat, we'll feed you through a tube until you can. I'm going to examine you now, and when I'm finished, we'll try the milk and cookies again. If you can't manage them, I'll put the feeding tube down, and then you can get some sleep if you like."

I grit my teeth at what I am about to see on a cursory physical examination. Breath sounds hard to hear through the scraping of protruding ribs against my stethoscope, but lungs seem clear enough. Heartbeat quick, but regular, no murmurs. Breasts shriveled like an old woman's. Abdomen sunken, withered, angry-red with scratches and the assaults of vermin. Bedsores over the sacrum open and deep; a piece of bone protrudes into the base of one of them. Skin everywhere flaking off from dehydration. I lift her into a sitting position, slightly nauseated by the limp compliance.

"Okay, let's try the milk again, Beth."

I hold the glass to her mouth and tilt it so the liquid touches her lips. She lets a small stream of white run down her chin. I try tasting it to show her it's safe, then experiment with a straw, a spoon, and a glass of juice. Angela calls me out to the phone, and when I return, the liquids have been spilled on the bed and floor, and Beth is lying in a pool of urine. Angela helps me clean up the mess and changes the sheets on the bed.

"All right, Beth, I think you've made yourself pretty

clear. I'm sorry about the feeding tube, but I guess that's the way it will have to be for now. I want you to be very clear about one thing from the start—I will not allow you to starve yourself to death. You are going to live, and one of these days, let's hope you'll even want to."

I send for a Levine plastic feeding tube and pack it in ice to ease the discomfort of insertion. Angela readies the table with lubricant and irrigating syringe.

"Okay, let's get this over as quickly as possible. It isn't pleasant, but it won't hurt you. Let me explain what I'll be doing and what you can do to make things easier. This is a flexible plastic tube with holes in one end. The tube will go into a nostril and down through the back of your nose and throat into your stomach. Once it's in place, you won't feel it. The only uncomfortable part will be the beginning. And what you can do to help is to swallow as soon as you feel the tube in the back of your throat. If you can do that, you won't gag, and the tube will go down more smoothly. Okay, here we go now. . . ."

Angela steadies Beth's head from the other side, and I begin the procedure. Beth grimaces silently, and tears flow down her cheeks from irritation of her nasal mucosa, but she swallows as instructed, and the ordeal is over in relatively short order. I tape the tube in place, apologize for the unpleasantness, and tell her I know what it's like, I've had it done. *Remembering how Ben and I choked and sputtered as we passed tubes on each other in medical school: "Stop it already, you're killing me!"*

Angela makes her comfortable and tucks in the sheets. I brush some hair back from her forehead and say to the passive face, "Sleep well, Marybeth Sloan. I'll come to see you in the morning and we'll see if we can make a beginning."

Back in the nurses' station, I write orders for Sustagen tube feedings and water, calculating out the calories and cc's needed in each twenty-four-hour period to keep a

woman alive who weighs eighty-four pounds and stands
four feet ten inches tall.

"Dr. Benetar?"

I look up at a balding man in overalls and thick, rimless
glasses.

"My name's Herb. I'm a patient here and I'm a friend of
Elaine's. We knew each other at Manhattan State; you're
her doctor, right? I saw you with her this morning. She
looked pretty out of it before you came; I tried to talk to
her, but she was too into herself, I guess. Anyway, I just
went out on a pass and brought back some pizza for the
others. Won't you come in and join us? There's plenty of
pie."

We walk together to the day room, and Herb pulls out
a chair for me. Hands shaking, a jowled, middle-aged man
with telltale, alcoholic red-veined nose and cheeks cuts a
piece of pizza and slides the plate across the table to me,
smiling and then looking away guiltily.

"Would you like something to drink? No booze, unfortunately!" he says with false gusto.

"Jeanie, my girl," he calls over his shoulder into the
kitchen. "You're slipping, woman! Bring in the soda yet!"

A haggard, mousey-looking woman of about forty
shuffles in, slippers flapping, with a six-pack of soda and a
quart of orange juice. She sits down at our table and begins
to drink from the container of juice.

"Hey, that's not fair!" Herb says, and takes the drink
from her hand. She begins to cry, and Herb mumbles,
"Okay, okay! I just wanted to put it in a cup for you."

He places a paper cup in front of her and pours her some
juice. She holds it in both hands and noisily drinks it all.
Herb pours her another cupful, but Jeanie has become
preoccupied with a piece of mushroom on her pizza.

To my right, a young man has been sitting staring at his
hands, long hair combed neatly in front of his face. A
pretty teen-age girl sits down quietly next to him. He picks

up his plastic knife and fork, and uses them to part the hair carefully in front of his eyes. He stares at the girl and says, "Ophelia again," then looks questioningly at me and asks, "What're you in for?"

Herb giggles hysterically and tells him that I'm a doctor. The boy puts down his knife and fork and lets his hair fall back in front of his eyes with a quiet, "Yeegods!"

I return the question and ask what he's in for.

From behind the wall of hair come the words, "Breathing, baby. Ever try to breathe in this city? They'll get you every time. Been trying to suffocate me since I was born. 'New York is a summer festival.' Lefrak City's an asshole's carnival. Pure poetry. Or pornography. Shut up. Listen." And he lapses into silence.

The pretty girl stares at me wide-eyed. "Are you really a doctor?" she asks timidly.

"Yes, why?"

"I'd like to be a doctor someday."

Somebody giggles in ridicule. She pays no attention and goes on. "When I get better, I'm going to work very hard to get good marks in school and make up the time I missed. I tried to kill myself; that's why I'm here. I think that was stupid now. I won't do it again. . . . What's your name?"

"I'm Dr. Benetar. Judy Benetar. What's yours?"

"Norma Rodriguez. I'm fifteen, but I'm a grade ahead of where I should be. They skipped me last year because my marks were so good. They weren't so good this year because of some problems I've been having. But if I work hard, I'll be ready for college in two years and medical school in six." She glances at Herb, who is putting a piece of pizza on her plate.

He asks, "Have you always wanted to be a doctor, Norma?"

"Off and on. But never as much as now."

She looks over at me, and I ask her, "Why now so much?"

Norma takes a moment to reply, then says quietly, "So

I can help people be more comfortable with the fact that there aren't any answers."

"Except maybe inside themselves," I comment.

She nods, but before I can say more, there is a loud crash from the far corner of the room. We all start and look around to see a dark-haired, middle-aged woman in a long, expensive-looking black robe stumble over the table and lamp she has overturned in an intended assault on the TV, which is absurdly silent in its advertisement of a deodorant.

I hear Herb say softly, "Jesus, it's Joanne! I hope I didn't upset her by turning off the sound. I thought it would be nice to eat our pizza in quiet. She's a friend of Elaine's, too, Dr. Benetar."

The woman screams in rage and gets to her feet again. She looks around wildly and then makes a rush for the television. Angela, a tall, bearded male aide named Mario, and I reach her before she can pull it off its stand. Her fingernails scrape the screen and she struggles to get away from us.

"Look at that stupid face! Just look at it! Some empty-headed cunt smiling at her armpits and making a fuckin' fortune from it! Goddamnit, let me go! I just want to smash that face!"

Angela reaches behind her with her left hand and switches off the TV.

"Joanne, Joanne. Okay, it's okay now. Hey, come on, hon."

The woman stops fighting quite suddenly and her body goes limp. We walk with her back to her room, and she sits dully on the edge of her bed. On her dresser is a picture of a family and a station wagon. The man is tanned, round-faced, and blond. He wears khaki shorts, a red fishnet shirt, and sandals with white socks. In one hand, he holds a map which he clowningly waves at the photographer. The other hand rests on the shoulder of a tow-headed boy of about six, who squints restlessly against the sun. A serene-looking Joanne leans back on the car, arms folded, smiling, in white jeans and a blue Indian overblouse. Her shoulder-length black hair is combed neatly, parted in the middle. A younger boy, holding a ball, leans out the window of the station wagon, watching his brother. Part of a split-level house and a well-trimmed, even lawn make up the background of the photograph.

Joanne catches my eye and laughs hollowly.

"Two years ago," she says, "about a week before we left for California. Would you believe it, doctor?"

"Sure," I answer quietly, "I'd believe anything."

She takes out a cigarette, and Mario lights it for her. She takes a long drag, exhales heavily, and vacantly watches the smoke disappear. There are heavy, dark hollows under her eyes.

"Christ," she says to the room, "I wish I was dead."

Mario stays to talk with her at a sign from Angela. As the two of us turn to leave, Joanne adds heavily, "Sorry about the scene in there, Angela. It won't happen again."

"It's okay," Angela says reassuringly, "but I think maybe you'd better discuss it with your doctor tomorrow. Or if you want, you can rap to any of us."

"O God, always the same line: 'Discuss it with your doctor.' I'm so sick of words." She draws a breath and sighs. "Sorry. Yeah, sure, Angela. I'll talk to Dr. Brown tomorrow. Why the hell not?"

Mario pulls up a chair and we close the door softly behind us.

"Whew!" Angela says outside. "Scary as it was, I'm glad to see some of that anger come out for a change. She's been so into herself, she's been giving me the creeps. By the way, Judy, I don't know if anyone's told you, but Elaine's been visiting her almost every day. They seem to be close in a funny kind of way. I think they were in a day center together a while back. Anyway, I thought you ought to know. Joanne could really be bad news for Elaine. She needs her like a hole in the head."

"This is the first time I've seen Joanne, but I think

Elaine's mentioned her a couple of times. What's the story on her, Angela?"

Angela stops for a drink at the water fountain under a Degas print of dancers fluffy and fatigued from ballet practice.

"Well," she says, wiping her mouth with the back of her hand, "I'm sure there's more to it than meets the eye, and Joanne was probably full of pathology to begin with, but the little I know about what happened to her has turned me off on encounter-type therapy for a long time to come. Gee, I hope I'm not insulting anything you might believe in with that remark?"

She looks at me wide-eyed, and I have to laugh.

"Well, you can laugh," Angela says, "but a lot of doctors are really touchy about their work, and I don't know what your particular brand of psychiatry is."

"Neither do I, to be honest with you. It probably draws from just about everything I've learned and been exposed to, and I hope it's couched in some kind of common sense and feeling for human beings. But it's still growing and I guess I hope it always will be. Dogma, any kind of dogma, makes me feel oppressed. Anyway, I don't know what your reference to encounter therapy was about, but I know that just like any other form of therapy, it can be dangerous if it's improperly managed. Maybe even a bit more than some others, because it forces issues so quickly. What happened to Joanne?"

"Well, her whole psychiatric history, recorded, that is, started after that trip to California she was talking about. She and her husband, who's a publicity agent or something like that, decided to take their kids to the West Coast for a vacation, show them San Francisco and stuff. They were sort of upper-middle-class, pseudo-hip type people, and they'd heard and read all about various new therapies. And so, while they were out there, they decided to join and live with some group they'd heard about for a week or two.

Anyway, to make a long story short, Joanne was sort of 'it' in the group one day. They were all swimming during a break from some heavy session about 'control' or something, and Joanne had been pretty upset. Somehow, they decided they could 'help' her by illustrating the issue for her. In short, what they did was to form a circle around her in the pool and tell her to try to get out. At first, I guess things were okay, and she took it more or less as a game. But then, when she realized they meant it, she got more and more frantic trying to break out, and of course she couldn't. They were in there for over an hour, and she got so exhausted and hysterical, she damn near drowned. Finally, she gave up trying and stood whimpering and freaked in the middle of the pool. Well, I guess somebody decided she'd been helped by then, and they broke it up for that afternoon. They hugged her and told her she was great. The next day they did the same thing. She tried to kill herself at the end of the week. And she's been in and out of hospitals here in the city ever since."

"Where was her husband when all this went on?"

"That's almost the worst part." Angela shudders. "He was part of the happy circle," she says sarcastically, "and the kids were watching."

Again, the realization that all effective forms of therapy come down to people. I have seen well-run encounter groups and been impressed by the speed with which crucial areas of difficulty have been exposed and explored for an individual. But therein can lie the danger as well, as in Joanne's case. Had her group had a competent therapist in the form of a stable, warm, knowledgeable human being, that devastating situation would never have developed or reached the point it did. Or had Joanne, or the other group members, had more of a sense of autonomy, or had she had more trust in the validity of her own feelings, she might not have participated so blindly in her own disintegration.

Angela returns to the day room to reassure the members

of the pizza party, and I go in to check on Marybeth Sloan. Her regular breathing suggests that she is asleep rather than just close-eyed. She has not interfered with the feeding tube taped to her nose, and in fact sleeps with the free end of it in the palm of her hand. Her hair has nearly dried, and I find myself admiring Angela's talent as a beautician. Falling loosely over her face and neck, the hair now hides or diminishes some of the gaping hollows, and Beth looks almost pretty and appealing.

Eight hours later, too tired and strung-out to sleep, I lie propped up on an elbow in the doctor's on-call room and watch dawn envelop the city. For the first time, there is a sense of quiet. Even the traffic on the avenue has thinned to an occasional truck or taxi. The clouds are gone, and behind the low, gray buildings in the east the sky is streaked with pale yellows and whites.

Aimlessly, my mind picks up fragments of a night that has delivered up an endless stream of depressed, confused, and lonely people. Ambulatory psychotics afraid of the added darkness. A junkie, a "pill-head," and two alcoholics who made feeble attempts to commit suicide. A middle-aged, expensively dressed woman who had been in Freudian analysis for fourteen years and was so hopelessly introspective and dependent on her analyst, she became paralyzed at having to make a decision about a phone call in his absence and came to the e.r. for help; on one level, a casualty from the other end of the spectrum from Joanne's encounter experience, but with similar problems of autonomy and therapeutic mismanagement. An adolescent boy who'd been slipped LSD or something else at a party, clutching my hand and pleading with me to "make it go away!" Several hungry people looking for rest and shelter, even in a madhouse; shunted to psychiatry because they knew the right things to say about hearing voices and losing control.

One of them had taken pleasure in watching *me* lose control. Because after twenty minutes of fitful sleep, at 2:30 A.M., I had been called to see him, and he'd pulled an Uncle Tom routine on me.

"Oh, thas' right, doctor. Anything you says, doctor," he'd drawled, grinning continuously, "but I tells you I been hearin' dose voices, an' they tellin' me to kill myself. I'll go wherever you sends me, doctor. Anything you says. Yes, ma'am." And he bowed and shuffled around the room, looking dramatically at the ceiling.

Losing my professional cool, I had muttered through gritted teeth, "Listen, Mr. Potts, if what you want is to get yourself into a hospital, don't wander in at two thirty in the morning and wake up the doctor on call! Wander in sometime during the day or early evening and try to look a little more distressed. Frankly, I'm having a hard time believing you, and if you haven't guessed by now, I'm pretty pissed off! Now I have to go and wake up another doctor at whatever hospital I send you to in the Bronx, if you really live where you say you do, which I doubt. But I'm stuck, because I more or less have to take what you say at face value. But you know all about this by now, I'm sure."

At which he'd grinned even wider and responded, "Yes, ma'am. Whatever you says, doctor."

Later, there was a gentle elderly man on a pension who was afraid to go home to his room in Astoria because "the Mafia and the Communists" were waiting for him in the bushes in front of his building; he'd been wandering the city the whole day without eating, because his food stamps were in the house and he only had 30 cents in his pocket. And finally, a young girl appeared at the door of the office in a torn dress at 4:00 A.M. and said nothing at all.

Anxious, drawn faces, hands unconsciously telegraphing their own tales, someone toning over and over in a flat, emotionless voice, "Wait . . . wait" in a building with mirrors for windows and camouflaged exit doors opening onto blind fire escapes littered with cigarette butts, blood, candy wrappers, a black sequin handbag, styrofoam cups, and needles and syringes.

The phone rings, and the clockface says I have slept for a couple of hours.

"Dr. Benetar, it's seven thirty. You wanted a wake-up call. Good morning!" The operator sounds cheerful and rested.

"Good morning. Thanks."

Another hour and a half of official on-call duty, and then a routine day's work, to which Beth Sloan has been added. With luck, I can finish lunch and get home early for a nap and a long weekend.

I shuffle down to the bathroom and splash my face with cold water. It surprises me that, apart from my tousled hair, I still look fairly intact in the mirror. The hazel eyes that stare back at me look deceptively reasonable, if a little tired. Nothing in my face to betray the sense of unevenness, the loss of proportion I have begun to feel. Typically, after a night like this, I am aware of an enormous hunger for something solid and pedestrian, like a plate of bacon, eggs, and toast, and a steaming cup of coffee. I run a comb through my hair and descend to the cafeteria.

The place is almost empty except for a table occupied by several rather large, boisterous surgical residents, only two of whom I know by name. After a Puerto Rican short-order cook fills my tray with the longed-for breakfast and an open smile, Dr. Jim Frank, brimming with a good humor that is almost painful at this hour of the morning, holds out a huge, meaty hand and says loudly, "Ah! The shrink of the night! Come and join us screwed-up butchers!"

He pulls up a chair for me, and they resume a conversation about post-operative wound infection. I settle down unobtrusively to my eggs and bacon, listening with half an ear and nearly grateful for their concrete talk.

A thin-lipped resident with straight blond hair addresses

me icily. "It must be nice not to have to worry about things like that."

I look up from my coffee, surprised at his sudden hostility. "Like what? Infection?"

"Like life and death."

"Well, Dr. ——?"

"Wright, Pete Wright."

"Well, Pete, each to his own, I suppose. And in answer to your question, I guess it depends on what sort of life and death you're talking about. We deal with another kind."

"Oh, really?" he says venomously.

Before he can continue, Jim interjects with a serious, open face and wide blue eyes that are reminiscent of a Dutch painting, "Speaking for myself, I have to hand it to you people. I couldn't do it. I don't know how you make it through a night with all those crazies. Where do you find the patience?"

He takes a sip of coffee and continues, "Jesus, I walked through the emergency room last night to see some guy with an aneurysm, and the waiting room outside your office looked like a cross between the Bowery and the back ward of a state hospital. I'd rather work three days straight than do an hour of what you do."

Pete Wright stands up and says he has to get scrubbed for the operating room. He tries to make his parting remark sound casual and off-the-cuff, but his smile looks weak and ugly. "Like you said, 'each to his own.' Well, if you like working with the scum of the earth, I guess that's your problem."

He picks up his tray and saunters out of the cafeteria, one-handing his rolled-up napkin into a waste basket in the corner of the room.

The other doctors are all looking at their coffee cups.

Fred Ngoka, a round-faced Nigerian orthopedic resident, breaks the ice. "Don't mind him. He can't help it if he's on the social register."

We all laugh, and, encouraged, Fred offers to tell us about

a case that gave him some trouble on the orthopedic ward that involved both psychiatry and surgery.

He pauses and looks at me appraisingly. "Maybe I better not tell you this one. It might offend you even more."

"How much more can I be offended in one morning? Anyway, no cliff-hangers, please. It's bad for my nerves."

They laugh appreciatively.

Fred's face lights up. From the way the others watch him, it's clear that he's a good story-teller.

"Well, since you're twisting my head—my arm, I mean," he says and settles into a mock seriousness, "I had this seventy-one-year-old woman, Anthea Harris, with a fractured hip, who was keeping me up every bloody night I was on call trying to walk out of the place on her fracture."

Jim cuts in, "Trying to get away from *you*, no doubt!"

"Funny, aren't you? I want you to know you're talking to the best Nigerian orthopedist this hospital has ever known!"

He bows to the applause that greets this remark.

Fred looks at me and says, "Ignore them, poor slobs. . . . Anyway, I think this woman was out in left field, lady doctor, mostly because her head was somewhere else as a way of life, if you know what I mean. But I have to admit that another reason might have been that her serum electrolytes were at times—only at times, mind you—a bit out of whack. And maybe her blood sugar did a few flip-flops once in a while? So, much as I hate to say it, there may have been some *organic* basis for her behavior—"

"What!" Jim shouts, "The orthopedist of the century can't keep his patients in electrolyte balance? I don't believe it! Scandalous!"

"Quiet, child. Listen to a man talk, now." Fred pauses and swallows some coffee with an audible gulp. "Anyway, I would drag myself out of bed and bump into this woman in the hall, limping along, and I would ask her where she was going. Every night, she'd say the same thing: 'I've been told to get out of this railway station.' Half asleep, I would mumble back, 'Who told you that?' and she would answer, 'Jesus Christ, of course. Who else?' Well, forgive me, noble shrink, but after many nights of this sort of thing, trying to convince this lady that she had a broken hip and would do best to lie in bed and rest, I confess that I did something rather unorthodox."

He looks at me wistfully and I am obliged to ask him with a conspiratorial sigh, "Okay, Fred, what did you do?"

Fred clears his throat and straightens his tie. "Well, when the nurses called me for the hundredth time at two A.M. to tell me Miss Harris was trying to get out of bed again and had untied all her restraints, I asked them to put her on the phone. . . . In a few minutes, I heard her charming, china-cup voice at the other end of the line and said to her in my deepest Sunday-school tone, 'Anthea Harris?' She said timidly, 'Yes?' I said, 'This is Jesus Christ speaking.' Without the slightest sign of surprise, I want you to know, she said, 'Oh. Yes, of course. Is anything wrong?' I said, 'No. I just wanted to tell you that the railway station is in good hands now and it's okay to stay there for a while. In fact, you might even try resting in bed, as though there was a reason for it. Pretend you have a broken hip or something.' There was a little silence, as if she was taking it all in, and then she says, 'Yes. Right. Anything you say, Lord.' "

Fred stops talking. His friends are convulsed with laughter.

Trying unsuccessfully not to succumb, I ask in a choked voice, "What happened then, Fred?"

He smiles. "Nothing. She went back to bed and stayed there. Haven't had a call about her since."

The others are stuffing handkerchiefs in their mouths.

"And did you ever call a psych consult?"

"Oh, sure," Fred replies. "They came the next day and wanted to know why I'd called them. 'Just an elderly woman with a mild organic brain syndrome. Give Thorazine twenty-five milligrams q.i.d. for agitation if you have to, but she seems happy as a clam to me,' your colleague said. I defy you to keep a straight face, lady doctor."

Fred looks at me and starts to chuckle, and it's all over. The mirth is contagious and unrestrained, until Jim starts pleading for it to stop so he can breathe again.

"Son-of-a-bitch, Ngoka, you're out of your head!" he gasps, "How am I gonna make it through a whole residency with you?"

"Just call up Dr. Benetar here and she'll slip you a tranquilizer from time to time. You'll survive."

Then Fred turns to me and says good-naturedly, "I have to hand it to you, though. In all sincerity, you people have helped me with some really tough cases that couldn't be solved with a mere phone call from a clown—much as I hate to admit it."

They get up to continue their rounds, and Tom Travis, a shy, watchful resident who looks younger than the others, lags behind, fumbling with some notes in his pocket.

"Do you mind if I ask you something?" he says, when the others are depositing their trays on the conveyor belt.

"Well, I don't think I have a good, solid answer to anything in my head this morning, but shoot."

"You won't believe this, but I nearly went into psychiatry. I had a sort of double minor in psychology and philosophy in college and really dug it. And I liked the psych rotation in med school. But when I started applying for internships, I sort of made up my mind at the last minute to do surgery. I've always loved to work with my hands, and I'm good at it, I think. And I wasn't really sure I could handle—"

He looks around, embarrassed, to see where the others are, and calls to them not to hold the elevator.

"Anyway, what I wanted to ask you was whether your work makes a big difference in the way you feel—yourself,

I mean. I mean, if you spend most of your time working with people in emotional trouble, empathizing, trying to be in some kind of touch, does it make you feel any less—I don't know—alone?"

"That's a helluva question for a surgeon! And I don't know if the best time to ask me is after a night on call, but anyway . . ."

He smiles and offers me a cigarette and I decline.

"Anyway, I guess the simple answer is no, it doesn't make me feel any less alone. Maybe just more aware that we all are. And that comforts me a bit and possibly has made me a little more tolerant of differences in people, for whatever that's worth. . . . But why do you ask, Tom?"

He looks at his hands, which are long and slender, then shoves them in the pocket of his white jacket and says with sudden anger, "Because it's not enough sometimes—for me, anyway—to cut and sew and make rounds and dismiss every damn thing that can't be answered with a scalpel as not worth the time of day!"

"Why can't you do both?"

"Both what?"

"Think *and* be a surgeon. It's been done before."

He breaks into a grin. "Yeah, but it's hard!"

"Only if you take yourself very seriously. Only if you forget your sense of humor," I say gently, talking as much to myself as to him.

Part Two

The evening air at Kennedy is heavy with cold, jet pollution, and the chaos of too many people in motion. The woman behind the desk tells me that the Irish plane has indeed arrived on schedule, but that it's now in a holding pattern over the airport, and landing will be delayed for at least half an hour.

Pleased that I remembered to come prepared, I pull an Agatha Christie from the pocket of my coat and retire to the most innocuous-looking corner I can find in the International Arrivals Building.

Remarkably, nothing disturbs my reading for the first twenty minutes. Then a family of four deposit themselves and their belongings in the bank of plastic chairs across from me, and I sense an end to my relative peace. The pasty-faced father wears a knit jersey with an initial embroidered on the pocket and carries a set of golf clubs and a transistor radio which he holds to his ear. His sunken-eyed wife cradles a sleeping baby in her arms and watches anxiously and haggardly over a fat boy of about six who stands in front of her stamping his feet and demanding something in a petulant voice. She touches his arm and ineffectually asks him to sit down. He turns angrily on his heel and walks over to the chair next to me, pouting.

I take refuge in my mystery.

The boy begins to play with the standing metal ash tray between the seats and finally makes so much noise that I look up to see him sprinkling ashes on the chair. He grins at me coyly and then repeats the procedure, looking for some kind of approval.

"That's not funny at all. I suggest you clean it up."

The boy looks dumbstruck, and then his face crinkles into an ugly prune and he begins to cry. He runs back to his mother and buries his head in her lap. She soothes the back of his head with her hand and looks apologetically at me across the orange plastic table between us.

It's a relief not to have to be a shrink at all times. To allow myself the luxury, in this instance, of feeling annoyed, intruded upon, angry. Had any one of the members of this family or all of them come to me seeking professional assistance, I would have had to look beyond, seek to understand, search out causes, systems of interaction, unstated fears, hopes, affections and antagonisms, fantasies.

The little boy comes back and glowers at me. I shrug my shoulders and decide to wait by the gate downstairs. A large crowd of relatives and friends already gathered around the exit doors shows clear signs of annoyance at the delay. We all wait for nearly another hour, shifting from foot to foot and listening to metallic announcements in English, Spanish, and French.

When John walks through the automatic doors, his eyes find me almost immediately by some uncanny radar.

"Hello, you," he says, takes my hand, and continues walking without a break in stride. "How do we get out of this place?"

I lead him through the traffic and faces and December night to the borrowed car in the endless lot, and we get in. Feeling suddenly shy and adolescent, I put the key in the ignition and make an attempt to start the car.

A large, warm hand covers mine. "Stop. Let me look at you."

The hand moves up to my hair, and I rest my head against the palm. I watch the lined, leathery face and gentle brown eyes take me in. They miss nothing.

"You've been holding out on me in your letters," he says softly. "Been working too hard, haven't you?"

"No, not really. Just stayed up late last night thinking about you coming."

"Liar. Toughie. Oh, god, Judith, come here—"

The strangeness dissolves and we are there for each other again.

"Hey, you crazy poet, member of the board, and all that—"

"What, dear, dear woman?"

"Do you think we can untangle ourselves long enough for me to get you out of this parking lot?"

Clyde puts a paw on John's nose, and I open a bottle of wine.

"How hungry are you—for food, I mean?"

"Medium. You know, I think this crazy cat really remembers me. Where's Sam?"

"Hiding probably. Or sulking. He loses his sleeping place for the next several nights."

"Couldn't we accommodate him somewhere?"

"On a single bed? Well, maybe when it's not in motion. I suppose we'll have to sleep sometime. How's a cheese omelet?"

"Perfect. Oh, bloody! I almost forgot your present! Hold on a minute before you do any cooking. . . ."

John rummages through his suitcase, and I lean against the wall watching him, feeling erotic and happy. He disengages a large brown parcel from a few stray socks and handkerchiefs and presents it to me with both hands and a slight bow.

"Christ, it's so heavy, John! What is it?"

He smiles for an answer.

I open it on the coffee table and stare in disbelief.

"John, you're insane! A whole smoked salmon?! How are we going to eat all this? It's enough for an army!"

"Yes, well, we may just develop the hunger of an army,

you know. And I think the fragrance of the salmon will blend in nicely with the general atmosphere after a while."

He waits puckishly for a reaction, and when he gets it, hangs his head in mock shame. "Sorry, love."

"You're outrageous and obscene. And I'm going to fix us an omelet. Do you want some of this gargantuan fish with it?"

"Why not? It will set the tone—"

"John, stop it!—or you may not get fed at all."

"That's not a bad idea. Why don't you just leave the salmon on the table, and we'll eat the next time we find ourselves in the kitchen?"

Dawn breaks around the ivy geraniums hanging in the windows. I turn my head on the pillow and find John's eyes on me.

"How long have you been awake?"

"About an hour. I'm still on Irish time, you know."

"What have you been doing all this time?"

"Lying here watching you. Stupid of me, but I always forget how beautiful you are—body and soul."

"Wouldn't happen to be a little bit biased, would you?"

"Yes. A bit. But I'm also very perceptive and aware—as well as being handsome, dashing, lovable, dynamic, and a great artist, of course—and humble."

I kiss him softly. "Yes, I know all about that. It's all true, too."

"Oh, Judith, don't be absurd. It's still an enigma to me that you've loved me and love me. I don't know quite what you see in me, really. You must be crazy, woman."

"Must be. You know what they say about shrinks. Anyway, let's not get into a contest about who's the least worthy. We always run a close tie."

"Good idea. Let's talk about something more satisfying, like eating."

"My God, you must be famished! Is the salmon still on the table?"

"I doubt it. The cats have probably dragged it off and devoured it between them. By the way, that sounds good. How about some smoked salmon for breakfast?"

"Okay. Anything else?"

"Oh, maybe a few eggs, cheese, bacon, tomatoes, coffee, a side of beef; nothing too heavy."

"Right. Bagels and cream cheese, too?" I push back the covers on my side of the bed.

"Why not? Wait a minute, please."

He pulls me down along his body and wraps the sheet around us. We hold each other in silence and comfort.

"Oh, John, it's so good. And last night—"

"I know."

"Hey, what's going on down there?"

"Oh. Well, I think it's what you Americans might call a growing hard-on. If we're serious about this breakfast business, perhaps we'd better get up before something happens. I think we may need a few calories to see us through."

I find the salmon miraculously intact, carry it into the kitchen, and slice us each several thin pieces. John starts the coffee, puts out some bagels, cream cheese, and cherry tomatoes, and then rests against the refrigerator watching me fix scrambled eggs and bacon. We load the feast onto a large blue tray to which John adds the blossoming white African violet from the bathroom and sit down at the round table by the window.

"This table looks lovely. What have you done to it?"

"Oh, I covered it with a new India print to celebrate your visit. . . . John, where are you going?"

"I thought I'd bring in the salmon. It will look nice on that cloth; and I kind of like having it around."

He reappears carrying the salmon on a large platter which he has garnished with some parsley and tomatoes and deposits it tenderly in the center of the table.

"Now! To get down to some serious eating." He wolfs down some eggs and coffee and fish.

"Judith?"

"Yes?"

"Do you think we should put on some clothes?"

"If you insist. . . ."

"Oh, not at all. Just my Anglo-Irish training and all that. Thought I'd make a small effort at decorum. Wouldn't it be fun to have my students join us this morning, or perhaps the Board?"

"Mm-m," I manage to mumble, too busy with my breakfast to get caught up in the fantasy of some forty-odd scholarly people sharing the meal with us.

"Yum—good salmon, John! Thank you."

He leans over, caresses my face, and says softly, "Good eggs, too. Good coffee. Good woman."

Then he tilts back in his chair, gnawing on a bagel, contemplative, quiet, alive. The cats perch on the windowsill watching us eat. John is a big man, broad, muscular. Middle age becomes his expressive, intelligent face. His hands are large, strong, and graceful in motion. He rests them on the table and turns to me thoughtfully.

"Tell me about you. You look tired, but really very lovely. This psychiatry stuff suits you, does it?"

I suppress an urge to tell him about the degree to which I have had to shore myself up against long, empty nights, the quiet fear of staying in my apartment alone after it has twice been broken into, the steady, polite intrusions of men who have not interested me, or the ugly time one of them appeared uninvited and shed any pretense of politeness; interrupted in his fumbling assault by a downstairs neighbor asking wide-eyed if a cut on her hand would require stitching.

Instead, I reach over to the window to offer the cats a piece of salmon, avoiding his careful eyes, and say casually, "I'm okay. Working hard, as you guessed; reading, sleeping, masturbating, going to an occasional show."

I straighten up and wipe my hands on a napkin, glancing quickly up at his face. It is clear from his sober silence that my ruse hasn't quite worked, but before he can follow up on his thoughts, I ask about his family. Taken off guard, he blinks and shrugs his shoulders.

"They're well. My wife's busy with her choral society and gardening. Steven's enjoying his first term at college, Evan's painting up a storm, and Eleanor thinks she might like to take up the oboe, of all things! Last year political activism, this year the oboe."

He begins to butter another bagel, continuing, "I'm beginning to feel old, you know? Can't keep up with them anymore."

"That's absurd," I say softly, grateful that I have spared him the burden of my complaints, sensing the chronic fatigue he must feel after working a sixteen-hour day and then returning to a prim English wife who has never wanted more than a "provider" in a husband, soundly rejecting the sensuality of this sensual man whenever she could.

In good Anglo-Saxon tradition, Catherine and John had married in the late 1940s without knowing each other. And in good Anglo-Saxon tradition, they had stayed together for over twenty years and would probably continue to "for the sake of the children and society."

Catherine's early photographs showed a true English beauty, and her face had promised a potential for passion and real sharing. In his youth, John had been shy and idealistic, tender and warm. He had doubtlessly been overwhelmed when this high-complexioned minister's daughter had consented to be his wife. His few references to the first years of their marriage hinted at a profound disappointment in each other to which neither would admit. With time, the pain had grown less acute. They had dutifully brought up their children; shared meals, fortnight seaside holidays twice a year, and family crises.

The rest was unstated and untouched. Catherine had her housework, her church and civil activities, and her garden.

John had turned his sensuality to restless walks on the moors near his home with the children and to his developing poetry. His wife had not seemed to notice the things he had learned from it. In the meantime, their life had become a well-established routine, disturbed only by sudden illness or death of a relative—and for the last few years, by our affair, of which Catherine had been unaware to the present.

"What's absurd?" John asks.

"Your getting old. In case you hadn't noticed, you grow more beautiful as time passes."

"Stop this mush. You're interfering with my digestion. And who ever heard of a beautiful man?"

"Lots of people," I answer, swallowing some coffee, "though I must admit to not having met many personally besides you."

John grimaces and gets up from the table. He lumbers across the room and pulls two blankets off the unmade bed.

"Chilly," he says, and wraps me in one with a kiss on my forehead. Draping the other around his body like a serape, he sits down again and considers my face.

"Wearing you down a bit, isn't it?" he states, rather than really questions.

"What?" I ask, picking up a fork and pretending a sudden interest in the grain of the salmon.

"This meeting for a few days every three or four months. The uncertainty of the whole thing. The loneliness . . ."

He reaches for his coffee and repeats, "Isn't it, Judith?"

I shrug my shoulders. "I'm doing okay, John."

He takes the fork from my hand. When I look up, his eyes catch and hold mine, and his expression asks for more.

"What can I say, John? The times we have together, abbreviated though they are, are worth all the rest. I've never known anything like this before. It's special. It helps keep me alive. Of course, I get irritable and feel sorry for myself sometimes, but then I stop and think what I would have missed if we'd never met. That puts things back in proportion and then I'm all right again. Really, John, I'm okay."

He hands me back my fork and pours himself more coffee.

"Tell me," he says a little huskily, "what would you say to a patient in this situation?"

"It would depend," I reply noncommittally.

"On . . . ?"

"On what the relationship meant to them and on how much it added to or interfered with their ability to function."

"And you say you're functioning well?"

"Yup. So they tell me, anyway. Just got a super evaluation from the powers that be," I say and bite into my bagel.

As a seeming non sequitur, John says into his coffee cup, "Stubborn, thick-headed creature you are."

I look up in surprise and ask with some irritation, "What is it you *want* me to say, John?"

"Nothing. I just feel sometimes that I'm bad for you. Keeping you from things."

"Forgive me, but shit, John, are we going to have this conversation again?"

"Sorry," he says, offended.

"I don't know how else to put it to you," I say, putting my hand on his arm in a kind of apology, "but you're the only person who seems to have seen me as a whole person and doesn't fall for my 'Mother Earth' bit. Women's Lib talks about men objectifying women as sexual objects, but my problem seems to be getting objectified as big mama, who's always there for people, understanding, providing, with minimal needs of my own. Granted, somehow I 'set it up' that way, but if you were able to see through it, why hasn't anyone else? Except my shrink, of course. But it's certainly no accident that I went into the profession I'm in. The sexual objectification is sometimes there too, but mostly it's an offshoot of the other. What can I say, John? If I met anyone else who saw me multidimensionally, as you do, then maybe something meaningful would happen. But how can I talk about some nonexistent person to make you feel less guilty that you're not with me all the time?"

He frowns, and we finish the meal in silence. In four years, we have been unable to resolve the issues that hang in the air. John's importance and devotion to his work are unquestionable. His attachment to his family and country is in his genes and cultural training. For him to abandon them and come to the States would be to leave chunks of his soul behind. For me to go there would invite a scandal that could endanger all the things that are vital to him. Despite my repeated assurances that our relationship is as much my responsibility as it is his, John's guilt about keeping me from a more conventional arrangement gnaws at him continually. In times of restlessness and despair, we have made attempts to stop seeing each other which have been just short of laughable.

Or during moments of psychological self-appraisal and flagellation, I have told myself about the problem I must have with commitment, that the very nature of this "interim" relationship is what keeps it going, that if we really had the opportunity to live together, we'd probably shrink back from fear.

"Bullshit," Mel Bernstein had said in response at one session earlier this year. "I've seldom seen two people more committed to each other. And as for you in particular, may I remind you that, against heavy odds, you stayed with a troubled marriage for just over ten years, trying to work it out.

"Look, you and John have a problem. You'll either resolve it better than you have so far or you won't. But don't give me this self-denigrating stuff. It doesn't fit you anymore."

Taking advantage of our preoccupation, Clyde has stealthily moved from the windowsill to an empty chair near me. I look up just in time to spear the salmon with my fork before it slips off the table between two black paws. Caught in the act, Clyde looks at me in wide-eyed innocence, lets go claw by claw, and then turns and runs like hell. John and I laugh in relief, grateful to the cat for restoring our warmth and humor.

We clear the table, and John offers to help with the dishes. "You wash, I'll dry," he says, and puts the dish towel around his neck waiting for a plate. "Hold on, woman, you're losing your elegant morning gown," he adds.

As he readjusts my slipping blanket, I suddenly remember. "Jesus, John! I forgot to tell you one of the most important things! God, where's my head?"

"Stand still, will you, woman? You're coming apart at the seams here."

He secures the blanket while I stand impatiently, and finally grins with satisfaction.

"There! Splendid costume, if I may say so. Now, what is it you were about to say?"

"I'm writing a book!" I shout. "I've started writing a book! What do you think of that? I only have about fifty pages of it written so far, but even on that much, I already have an agent, and she thinks we can get a contract with a publisher without any trouble!"

"That's fantastic, Judith! How wonderful! In my own experience, it's rather difficult to get an agent so quickly. It must be very readable. What's it about?"

As we do the dishes, I tell him about how a morning of restless note-taking about patients I'd seen in the e.r. became an increasing desire to communicate something about myself and the work I do to the general public.

I hand him some dripping silverware and add, "I'd originally hoped to keep it sort of clinical, just describing and chronicling my work, but that felt somehow false and incomplete, and I guess I came to the realization that the way I work is inseparable from who I am as a person. So now it's partly documentary, partly autobiography, partly just, well, 'musing,' I guess."

John kisses my cheek and says, "Judith, I think it's really exciting! But again, speaking from my own experience, a kind of mixed blessing."

"Why?"

"Ah, because as challenging and thrilling as it may be, the torment of any artist is that the work of art never quite fulfills the original conception of it."

I pause and look up from the sink. "Hey, wait a minute! I didn't say this was going to be a work of art. It's more, I don't know, it's more pieces of information and experience that I'd kind of like other people to know about, that's all."

"There you go, putting yourself down already," John says, motioning for something else to dry. "Tell me, does this thing have a message?"

"I didn't start out meaning it to have one," I answer, giving him a cup, "but it looks as though I want to say something like 'psychiatrists are human, too,' or 'we're all in this thing of life together.' Something like that."

"Oh, I see. Then I'd say you have your work cut out for you. If you don't set yourself up as something special, like a priest, I'm sure people are going to want to see you that way, anyway."

"That's partly what I'm afraid of. But we'll see."

"By the way," John says and clears his throat, "do you plan to put me in this thing?"

I turn off the water and regard him seriously. "I'd hoped to, John, but I wanted to ask your permission first. Do you mind?"

Without warning, he lifts me up and carries me into the living room over his shoulder.

"I'd be delighted!" he laughs, slapping my bottom. "Just

don't make me into the depraved monster I'm about to be!"

We spend the rest of the morning by the fire, making love. In the afternoon, we walk through the park to the Metropolitan Museum and back again.

The next few days and nights are golden, gentle explorations of the city and each other, from which I reluctantly borrow an afternoon to check on the progress and status of some of my patients and attend a required conference.

Although the staff has been taking her daily to community meetings in a wheelchair, Beth has remained uncommunicative. Her fragile body has been kept alive by tube feedings and total, twenty-four-hour nursing care. Because there are potentially dangerous complications from leaving a feeding tube in place too long, I have been under increasing pressure to transfer Beth to a state hospital, where she can receive electroshock treatment in hopes of bringing her out of it. In the recent past, shock treatment could have been administered at West End General also, but Dr. Faulkner has just issued a memo stating that no patient under the auspices of the department of psychiatry of West End General Hospital is to have shock treatment without his or her written consent, and Beth is not about to consent to anything. The memo goes on to say that if it is felt that the only appropriate treatment for the patient *is* electroshock, then the patient must be transferred to another facility where they can make their own decision about the procedure of choice.

Although I agree with Dr. Faulkner in principle, I do not want to lose Beth to a state hospital and find myself in a curious bind. After days of grappling with the problem of her severe allergy to any of the medications that might have helped her, I decided to try to reach her without artificial aids and resolved to spend at least an hour a day with her, utilizing various approaches, which included reading her

The Little Prince and other books; guessing from what her
parents had told me over the phone and in separate interviews about what might have precipitated her withdrawal;
pointing out the situation to her that had been set up between her, me, her parents and the staff; sitting in silence
listening to music; and sharing odd bits of neutral small
talk with her.

The Friday before John arrived, I explained to Beth that
I would be away a few days and that I would see her briefly
before my official return to work. That same day, a
majority of the staff voted to transfer her to a state hospital
if she had not begun to eat in another week's time. Feeling
choked and unhappy, I had decided to share with Beth the
staff's decision and the bind I felt she had put me and
herself in.

My parting remark to her had been, "Well, Beth, I think
you ought to understand that there's no such thing as a
truly 'passive' action on your part, especially now. Even if
you decide to continue not to eat, I want to point out that
it will essentially be your decision to go to the state hospital. Whatever happens is up to you."

Earlier in the same week, I had had to admit Elaine to the
same ward after her friend Joanna jumped from the roof of
the outpatient building. Ironically, Elaine had been doing
really well before Joanna's suicide; she had been working
as a volunteer in the hospital, taking a remedial English
course at night, and thinking about writing a book about
herself. When she heard of the suicide, she had begun to
hallucinate almost immediately. Treek told her that she
was responsible for what had happened.

"You're all poisonous and contagious, you bitch. That
woman caught your poison and was *driven* off that roof, do
you hear?"

Elaine then had decided she'd better do something about
her poison, before anyone else was affected. She put hot
compresses over different parts of her body to "draw the

poison to the surface," as she put it, and then "let it out" with a kitchen knife. I'd been called at home that night by a surgical resident from the e.r. after they'd finished stitching up her skin wounds. Since her admission to the ward, for the most part, she'd been ominously quiet and superficially compliant.

I arrive at the hospital just in time to make the required conference, dreading the monotonous monologue that will ensue. I sit in the corner at an angle, where I can look out the window and daydream about John, feigning an expression of concentration and catching threads of Dr. Hilton Jenks' case presentation and Freudian analysis of it.

When I hear a factory whistle nearby, I realize that the hour has passed more quickly than I'd expected. I wait for Dr. Jenks to dismiss us. He stubs out his cigar on the overflowing aluminum ash tray. The conference room is close and uncomfortable and filled with heavy, stale smoke.

"So we see here, too, as in other case examples over the past months"—he folds his pudgy hands on the table in front of him—"how the Oedipal complex, unresolved, can lead to serious neurosis in our little boy, a neurosis that may require years of careful analysis. . . . Are there any questions?"

I glance around the room. Helga is catnapping behind her hand; most of the others are restless and anxious to be dismissed.

"Doesn't *anyone* have a question to ask me?" Dr. Jenks glares at us over his thick glasses.

I make a quick decision and raise my hand.

"Well, yes, what is it?" Dr. Jenks looks even more annoyed to have received a response.

"I had a question about the advice you gave to the boy's mother."

"Yes, well, go on, Dr. Benetar, go on—"

"You said that you told her not to have any more men sleep with her in the house, because, if I understood you correctly, even if the boys didn't see them making love, it would arouse competitive feelings and castration anxiety in the children."

"That's right. And fairly obvious, I think. So what's your question?"

"What did the mother do then?"

"What do you mean, 'what did the mother do then'?" He looks at me incredulously.

"Well, for a sex or a love life? Her husband was living with another woman, she had two small children to take care of, her funds were limited, she was young and attractive and alone. So if she followed your advice and no longer had men friends at the house, what did she come up with as an alternative for her own emotional and sexual gratification?"

"How should I know? The boy is my patient, not the mother."

Alan Goldberg throws me a warning glance, but I decide to see it through.

"But Dr. Jenks, wouldn't the child's emotional well-being be threatened if the mother were frustrated and unsatisfied?"

The child psychiatrist takes off his glasses in dismissal. "In the future, when I ask for questions, ask me something relevant to what's being discussed. Any problems you people may have about Women's Lib and the like, take up with your own therapists. That's all for today."

Stung, I walk out to the corridor with the other residents. I feel an arm around my shoulder and look up to see Alan smiling and shaking his head.

"I tried to warn you, Judy."

"I know, Alan, but God—"

"Yeah, yeah. I know," Alan nods, "Sometimes you feel you just have to say something in there. Me too. But just think what you tried to take on, for Christ's sake. Hilty Jenks is the *original* male chauvinist pig. He's been at it for fifty years, at least. You really think anything you say is gonna make any difference to him?"

He looks at my face and says, "You okay? I gotta run to see a patient."

"Yes, sure, Alan. Thanks. See ya."

He waves and hurries down the hall, coat trailing over his arm, galoshes flapping.

I start for the elevator and nearly run down Dr. Faulkner, who is leafing through a periodical outside his office. I excuse myself and turn away hastily.

"Hey, hold on there, Dr. B."

When I turn back, the chairman of the department takes me in at a glance and says, "What's your hurry?"

"Oh, I have a couple of patients upstairs I have to check on, and I'm really on vacation for a few days."

"I see. Got a few seconds you can spare before you go up?"

"I guess."

"Good. C'mon in for a minute."

He holds open the door to his office, and I sit down in a large, vinyl-covered beige chair. Dr. Faulkner pulls up another one and smiles at me.

"Is anything wrong?" he asks quietly. "You look kind of —how shall I say—discombobulated. Did something happen?"

I shift in the chair and the vinyl squeaks. "No, not really," I say uneasily, "I just came from Dr. Jenks' conference."

Dr. Faulkner sits back knowingly and grins. "Ah, that explains it! What happened in there today?"

I tell him, and he chuckles to himself.

"Well, what did you expect?" he says finally. "I'm a little surprised you let yourself get sucked in."

I make a gesture of frustration and grumble irritably, "I

don't know. I just don't know how to deal with him sometimes. It's intolerable. He's so damn provocative!"

It flashes through my mind that what I find provocative
about Dr. Jenks is not merely his classical Freudian point
of view, which is important to understand, even if I disa-
gree with much of it. It is also, and perhaps even more so,
his *attitude* about his orthodoxy, which borders on fanati-
cism and closes him off to possibilities for growth or expansion.

"Want some advice?" Dr. Faulkner volunteers.

"Sure."

"Deal with him the way you might with any person or
situation that's troubling."

"I'm not sure I follow you."

"To solve a problem, one objectifies it, steps back from
it, gains a broader perspective. So objectify Hilty Jenks!"
Dr. Faulkner chuckles.

"Sounds reasonable enough to listen to you talk about
it," I admit, "but I'm not sure I could sustain it. Do you
realize I have to go to that conference twice a week for
another five months to complete the requirement?"

"So use your objectivity to write a paper then. Call it"
—Dr. Faulkner laughs at his own humor—"call it something like 'The Dying Breed.'"

He looks at my face and says, "Oh, come on, Judy, cheer
up! You'll survive. If a person wants to get somewhere in
life, in a career, in whatever, some percentage of his or her
waking hours is going to be spent having to deal with a
certain amount of shit. There's no way out of it. If you're
not prepared to make some compromises, very often you
end up on one of the psych wards yourself."

He draws a breath and continues, "That doesn't mean
you have to submit to anything unacceptable in your head.
You wouldn't, anyway. But the plain and simple fact is that
if you're ever going to get to a place where you can exercise
your rather considerable talent usefully, that means ac-
cumulating a certain number of 'brownie points.' And un-

fortunately, one of those brownie points is completing Hilty Jenks' course. End of speech."

I thank him for his time and concern and get up to leave.

"Anytime," he says. "Come in and rap whenever you feel like it. I'm happily available for that kind of thing."

Dr. Faulkner pauses with his hand on the doorknob, as though remembering something. "By the way," he asks, "how are you doing with that catatonic woman?"

"Beth Sloan? Not too well, I'm afraid. It's come down to the wire. She has two more days to start eating before I have to initiate transfer proceedings for probable shock treatment."

He puts his hands in the pockets of his tweed jacket and ponders for a minute. "Let me ask you something. Why don't you just let her die?"

"What!" I look up in disbelief.

"Don't be so shocked. It's a philosophical question, but an important one."

"But the answer is obvious, isn't it?"

"Is it?" He smiles enigmatically.

"Well sure, I think so. She's another human being in serious trouble and she needs help. Besides which, this particular woman happens to also be young, intelligent, and she has a potential for functioning well."

I pause, perplexed, not understanding the direction of Dr. Faulkner's inquiry.

He folds his arms and says, "That may all be true. But it's also true that she's an adult and she's made a decision to withdraw and die. Why do you want to deny her that decision?"

"Because, well because"—I search for the right words— "she's not competent to make that decision. It's an irrational, distorted choice."

"That's your opinion. What about hers? What about her rights? How do you know she wouldn't be better off dead? Who are you to question her choice?"

"A doctor with a little training in psychiatry."

"Yes. And doesn't a doctor treat people who ask or want to be treated? Isn't your forced feeding and your forced presence an imposition on the privacy of this woman, who has neither solicited nor in any other way indicated her desire for it?"

I rub my forehead, feeling taken unawares and unprepared to question my motives.

"Yes, I guess it is an imposition in a way. And I have to admit, Dr. Faulkner, that it troubles me a little now and then. But it's for her benefit, isn't it? I mean, she would just die without treatment, like the catatonics in the old days."

"So I ask you again, why don't you just let her die, if that's what she wants?"

He moves one of the vinyl chairs back to its place.

"I couldn't stand to just sit back and watch her die!"

He wheels around and says, "Aha!"

"Oh. Yes, I see what you're after, now. And it's true. Part of why I'm doing what I'm doing is that, for whatever reasons, I can't handle the guilt and anxiety that this other person's withdrawal or act of craziness evokes in me."

Another thought that has often plagued me prompts me to add, "And I think there may also be a certain amount of vanity and grandiosity involved on my part. I mean, it's like I'd 'get my kicks' from being the one who could bring this woman out of the woods."

"Well," he says, "don't put yourself down too much. We doctors and shrinks are all pretty much alike in one respect. It takes a while to realize that we're as dependent on our patients for a kind of definition as they are on us."

"Then what's the difference between us? It doesn't seem to convey much to say that they're 'sick' and we're 'well.'"

"That's really a very pertinent question," he says, leaning back against his desk. "Let's take Beth for an example. You can't tolerate the withdrawal, the wasting away, the lack of communication, the unrelatedness from her, and it makes you feel you want to do something about it. She *can* tolerate it, in fact, has chosen it in preference to having to relate to people. Your intolerance of your own distress is in part why you're the 'doctor' and she's the 'psychotic.' You feel you have to work it out, take action. She doesn't, at this point at least. It's a bit different with 'neurotics' like you and me, who come for therapy because they can't tolerate *their* anxiety and are asking for help with it. There you feel you have something more familiar to relate to."

"I see what you're saying, but you make it sound like a conscious choice on Beth's part. I'm not sure how much of this is really under her control."

"And you never will be. Nor will anyone else, probably including Beth," he speculates, idly playing with a crystal paperweight. It has begun to snow outside the window behind his desk.

"But," he continues, "control, now that you mention it, is another interesting issue to think about and fairly central to doing effective psychotherapy. Also to learning and human relatedness."

"Could you say something more about that, Dr. Faulkner? I remember a session with Elaine a few weeks ago when she was being pretty infantile and defiant. She said, yes, in fact, she actually said she felt great because she was in control. Could we go a little further with it?"

He laughs and says, "Sure, if you don't mind me throwing a few of my own pet notions at you."

"I'd be delighted."

"Well, in essence, what you're saying to Beth is 'submit to me and it will be worth your while.' "

"How am I asking her to submit to me?"

"By asking her to eat, to go to the bathroom, to communicate, to begin to speak a common language—because you want her to. Right now, she has you and a whole staff of nurses and aides feeding her, caring for her, wiping her rear after she soils herself, and so on. Conscious or unconscious, she's in complete control, demanding total care—

and getting it—by playing on your intolerance of your own feelings about the situation. Now you can speculate, with good reason, that it's her way of making up for the care she never had, but I don't know how much that helps you with management or resolution. It's certainly effective, I guess you'll agree. . . . How long could you or I stand to watch anyone lie around in their own shit without doing something about it?"

The snow blows against the pane and we both watch it for a moment.

"So in essence, then, what I'm doing with Beth is trying to reason, cajole, seduce, threaten, or bully her into being uncomfortable enough so that she's willing to 'speak my language.' And then maybe I can get a clue as to what went on before she got to this point and work on it with her."

"More or less," he says sympathetically. "It's a mammoth task. And interestingly, or paradoxically, it's a task for which young, zealous residents in training are often better suited, with their beginning enthusiasms and idealistic hopes of 'curing' even the most seemingly hopeless patients. Those enthusiasms get transmitted to the patients and often seem to do as much good as years of professional experience."

"What if I lose with Beth?"

He draws a deep breath. "Then she'll go off to some state hospital where they'll probably, as you said, shock her head. As you know, it's the treatment of choice for catatonia, according to most authorities."

"Yes, I know. I have my own uncomfortable feelings about shock treatment, but I don't know if they're rational. Dr. White, at least, and a lot of respected psychiatrists say that where shock is indicated, people really get better without any ill effects. In my own experience on the wards, the only person I've seen significantly improved by it was an elderly man with a psychotic depression."

"Maybe so," Dr. Faulkner sighs. "Personally, I question the 'getting better' part. I'd speculate that if people seem to come around, it's because the shock dulls their minds enough that they don't remember or can't relate on a feeling level to whatever's hanging them up. And I suppose that's one way of approaching it. But not here in this hospital, not without the patient's knowledge or consent. Not while I'm here, anyway."

"Forgive me, but isn't that just passing the buck?"

"Possibly," he says, "but not necessarily. The doctors in the state hospitals also, theoretically, have a freedom of choice about what they'd want to do with Beth."

Troubled, I search for the words to pinpoint my confusion. "Dr. Faulkner, can I pose a hypothetical situation for a minute?"

He laughs. "Sure!"

"Supposing you were 'it,' Beth's *last* doctor, the one who received her in the state hospital, and she were clearly going to die, and there were no other place to send her and the only thing that hadn't been tried was shock. What would you do?"

Without hesitation, he says, "I'd shock her."

"Why?"

"For a couple of reasons—one, because of some of the things we've been talking about, that is, how I would feel about letting her die. And two, because under the law, I could be sued for negligence for not trying every possible means to keep her alive."

He puts a hand on my shoulder as he shows me out.

"I can empathize with you, Judy, if that's any consolation. But I realize that you residents are the ones on the front lines dealing with the nitty-gritty. One of the advantages of being an administrator in my position is that I seldom, if ever, have to come face to face with those things anymore. Except in my head, of course, and that's a little different qualitatively. Where are you off to now?"

"Three guesses—I'm off to see Beth Sloan. It may be my next-to-the-last day with her."

"Good luck," he says, and turns to respond to a question from his secretary.

Mulling over our conversation, I leave Dr. Faulkner's office and head for Castle 12, feeling puzzled and curious about the work I've been doing with Beth. Essentially, the role the staff and I have been playing with her on a nonverbal level has been that of a good mother caring for a helpless infant. Verbally, we have been appealing to the part of her that has, in the recent past, been able to function as an adult, the part that brought her as far as a master's degree in biology. Without an articulated response from her, it has been hard to know what impact, if any, some of the things we've said to her have had.

My own feelings about her general lack of response have varied from a kind of clinical tolerance to a pained empathy to frustration and anger at times, often with an accompanying guilt at my apparent lack of effectiveness.

Thinking back over the conversation with Dr. Faulkner, I find myself questioning the investment I have made in time and energy trying to reach her. All the things we talked about may account for it in part, but I would like to think that on some level, one of the major factors in my concern is an identification of sorts. I would like to believe that although we may not express our trouble or despair in the same ways, we have enough in common on some human level to be able to communicate significantly through some shared idiom or experience. Work with Elaine has reinforced my hope that our ability to speak a common language at times may be true with other people labeled psychotic as well.

Clara greets me at the nurses' station with a twisted smile. She clowningly ushers me in and closes the door. "Well, lovey, do you want to hear about me first or your two kiddies camped out up here?"

I sit down heavily on the nearest piece of available counter space. "From the look on your face, Clara, I think I'd rather hear about you first."

"Good choice!"

She beams and pirouettes and says, "How do I look?"

"Thinner, I think. You've lost weight."

Clara applauds herself. She bubbles happily, "Right! You noticed! I've lost twelve pounds in the last two weeks. It shows, hurray! I bought myself this outfit to celebrate. I'm down to a size fourteen. Like it?"

I look appraisingly at the white wool pants suit and answer, "Yeah, it's super. But not very practical for work, is it?"

"No, but I just felt so good I had to wear it this afternoon. I'll keep it for evenings after this."

She remembers and asks, "And how are you? Bowlegged yet?"

"Clara! I'm surprised at you! I haven't the faintest idea what you're talking about, besides."

She pretends to hide behind a hand and giggles.

"Jesus, you really are hypomanic today, nurse! What are you doing to those poor patients? Anyway," I add casually, "I hope I have a little more stamina than that! By the way, I'd kind of like to get back to John. Tell me what's going on with Beth and Elaine."

Clara gets serious and businesslike. "They're pretty much the same, really. Elaine's doing a lot of staring into space and not much talking to anyone. She's been asleep for the last half hour. I don't think she's been sleeping much at night. Maybe you could increase her sleep meds a bit? She really looks haggard."

I nod and she goes on, "The look on my face when you came up was about Beth. Fran and I had just finished cleaning up after her. Nothing new, really. But she pulled a real cutey today! You know we've been giving her a bedpan every couple of hours, hoping to catch her at the right time.

Well, just before you arrived, Fran had put her on it.
. . . So, I go in about ten minutes later, she hands me the
empty bedpan with her eyes closed so she won't have to
look at me, turns away, and then shits in the bed. It was a
massive b.m. too, and we've been up to our elbows cleaning
it up. Anything else you want to know?"

"Sounds like you had fun."

"Yeah, you doctors ought to try it sometime. Builds character."

"How are her vital signs, to change the subject?"

Clara fishes for the chart and reads off, "Blood pressure
ninety over seventy, pulse eighty-six, respirations eighteen,
temp ninety-nine. Nothing exciting."

"Tube feedings going okay?"

"Yup."

"Has she made any attempt to eat or drink on her own?"

"Nope."

"Okay, thanks, Clara. I guess I'd better go see her," I say,
struggling to my feet. "Well, here goes nothing."

In the hall, I bump into Joel Kent walking out of one of
the patient bedrooms.

"Hey, what's up, Joel? You look like you want to slug
somebody."

"I do, but I'm not sure who," he snarls. "Adrian just
admitted this seventy-six-year-old woman from the emergency room. I don't know how medicine talked or conned
him into it. Granted, she's hallucinating. But God knows
why, maybe she has a brain tumor. But anyway, hallucinating's the least of her problems. She's a major medical
handful, with a catheter in her bladder, an intravenous in
her arm, and trouble walking. The nurses will freak out.
They're just not equipped to handle her on a psych floor,
especially now, with your prize in the quiet room. And
she's got two roommates who'll be kept up all night with
her moaning—just what they need to help get their heads
back together!"

"Has she ever been a psychiatric patient before?"

"No, of course not. She's just been gradually getting old and senile and a little belligerent and a little paranoid, and her family got fed up with her and decided they'd let her shift for herself in her hotel room for the last month," he fumes. "So naturally, left to herself, she got good and sick, and they dumped her on the hospital. And medicine dumped her on us."

He looks at the ceiling in frustration and wails, "So what, pray, am I gonna do with her! Get her well enough to send her to a nursing home where she'll get sick all over again and probably die? You're right, Judy. I *would* like to slug somebody. Know any likely candidates?"

I have the feeling of having had this conversation many times before. About how there's no place for the elderly in our culture, so they feel useless, get sick, and end up in the hospital, where medicine and psychiatry fight over who'll be primarily responsible and who'll make the final disposition to the nursing home. A sense of futility stops me from saying to Joel that maybe it's society he should slug.

I look in first on Elaine, who appears to be sleeping soundly with her thumb in her mouth. Since it is not her regular appointment day, and she has not been expecting me, I decide not to wake her and turn toward the quiet room.

Fran emerges with an armful of foul-smelling sheets and blankets, a cigarette dangling from one corner of her mouth. "She's all yours!" she says emphatically. "Have a ball!" and stomps off to the laundry chute.

Beth is sitting up in bed examining her nails when I walk in. She sees me, drops her hands, and closes her eyes. The nurses have clipped the free end of the feeding tube to the shoulder of her hospital gown. Non-irritant tape is wound around the portion entering her nose and anchored to her nostrils to keep it from slipping. She has gained a little weight from the tube feedings and vitamin supplement and has begun to look appealing and attractive with her Angela-styled shag-cut.

I pull a chair up to the bedside, feeling a growing sense of despair at her impending transfer.

"Hello, Beth."

We sit in silence for several minutes.

"Well, I don't think I have much to add to anything I've already said. Perhaps we'll just sit together for a while. We've finished two books, but I think it's pointless to start another one now, if I have to begin transfer proceedings tomorrow. I don't have anything else to say about that, Beth. I think you know what the choices are. I'd just like to reiterate that I hope you don't choose to define yourself as a chronic, long-term mental patient. I think you'll miss out on a lot if you do."

I sigh tiredly and add, "But it's your choice. I can't make it for you. I can work *with* you, if you decide to stay, but I can't make the basic decision *for* you."

Beth keeps her eyes closed and picks fretfully at a hang-nail. She sneezes, but ignores the tissue I hold out to her. I leave it on the covers, and when she sneezes a second time, she snatches it up quickly and blows her nose. Watching her annoyance and obvious discomfort as she wipes the tissue around the tube gives me an idea that seems worth a try. I switch on the portable radio I have loaned her and we sit for another twenty minutes listening to Mozart.

When the music gives way to an automobile commercial, I stand up. "Well, Beth, I'll have to leave in a few minutes."

As usual, the only visible response is a flicker of eyelashes.

"You know, it occurred to me that you can't have had a full night's sleep since you've been here, if you've been getting the tube feedings every four hours around the clock. Supposing I take the tube out now, and you have at least one good night's sleep without it. And maybe if you're more comfortable, you can think more clearly about the things that have happened to you, the different alternatives, and some of the decisions you have to make. If you're able to eat during the next twenty-four hours, great. I won't have to start transfer papers, and we can go on from there. If, on the other hand, you can't or won't eat, very little will have been lost. I'll just put a new tube down tomorrow morning. But at least you'll have had a rest from it. Okay? Let me just get some tissues here and take this nasty thing out of your nose. . . ."

I undo the tape and clip, and, with a handful of tissues in each hand, start to remove the tube as quickly as possible to minimize the discomfort. Beth coughs, gags, and sneezes as I drop the caked plastic tube and tissues in the waste basket. She keeps her eyes closed, but takes a tissue from me and blows her nose again. Then she puts her hands at her side and sits motionless and rigid, waiting for my next move.

"Okay, I'm off, Beth."

I pause at the door on my way out. "By the way, at the risk of being repetitive, I want to say again that there's no such thing as being passive in this situation. Even if you decide not to eat, that's an active decision on your part, which will mean continued tube feedings, fairly rapid transfer to another hospital, and, most likely, shock treatment. Again, it's up to you. Incidentally, it's snowing out. If you ever decide to open your eyes and get up and look out, it's really quite lovely to watch coming down over the city.

"Well, see ya," I say flippantly, "Hope you make the right choice for yourself."

I find Clara, give her a quick progress report, and suggest that she merely notify Beth when the meals come up from the main kitchen, but avoid getting into any overt power struggles with her about food.

"Gotcha. Will do," she says. "Hey, where are you running in such a hurry?"

"I'm late for an appointment over in the outpatient department. Take care, skinny! See you soon." And I get on the elevator.

Just making the light, I run across the street to the outpatient department, experiencing a certain relief that my next hour and a half will be spent with verbal, "neurotic" people, who have at least made a clear choice to try to grapple with the things that hang them up. That choice in itself is half the battle, i.e., being discontent with oneself and wanting to do something about it. The rest is a matter of defining the problems and, with a certain amount of insight and understanding, either exploring other ways of coping and relating, or at the very least, deciding that they are important for one reason or another to one's life style and accepting them with a greater degree of tolerance.

I stop briefly at the secretary's desk to check the office I've been assigned today. The hospital has been in the process of painting and de-roaching the outpatient building, and my room assignment has changed from week to week. This week, at least, I have the luxury of seeing my two outpatients, Stan Morris and Nancy Klein, in the same place.

Stan, a college student I've been seeing for about six months, had been referred to our clinic by his family g.p. after he'd freaked out on an acid trip. It had frightened him enough to actually make the move to call for an appointment. The sessions had been stormy and tedious in the beginning. Stan had been into a heavy drug scene, and had resented having to talk to "some straight broad, who doesn't even know where it's at."

But he'd continued to come, missing a few appointments here and there, often coming late, sometimes leaving early, but coming for half a year so far, moving in leaps and bounds at times, stagnating and refusing to deal with anything at others.

His tall, lanky figure dwarfs the cramped office. He stretches his long, studded-jean legs in front of him and nods through tinted, rimless glasses at the window.

"Great view you've got here," he says.

I glance at the filthy pane facing out on an even filthier airshaft.

"Yes," I agree, "it's a pretty dreary room. As soon as they finish painting the offices, we're supposed to have a permanent place assigned to us, presumably more cheerful than this."

"What if it isn't?"

"Well, then we'll have to do something about it."

"Like what?" he asks laconically.

"Oh, put up some posters, maybe do a mural on the window. We'll think of something."

"Yeah, sure," he says, losing interest. He starts fingering his beard. "I nearly did some acid again this week. Yesterday, in fact," he mumbles.

"What stopped you?"

"Oh, shit, I don't know," he says, and puts one foot up on the low table. "I had some stuff to do for my ecology course, I guess was one thing. And I never would've made it here today if I'd taken that shit."

He opens the pocket of his denim shirt and pulls out a pack of cigarettes. I hand him an ash tray from the table.

"Surprises me a little," he goes on. "A month ago maybe, if that had happened, I would've probably taken it anyway. But I just couldn't get into that scene last night; they were all tripping and blowing their minds, and I just couldn't get into it with them."

"Why not? What do you think has changed?"

He looks over at me briefly for the first time. "I don't know. Something seems different, but I just can't put my finger on it."

"Well, we've met often enough now and talked a lot about what drugs do and don't do for you and just lightly touched on some of the reasons why you might have started taking them in the first place. So where are you at with all that now?"

"Whew, this is so heavy!" he says. "I don't even know where to start. I *do* know I've been thinking a lot about my parents lately, but I can't tie it all in."

"What about them?"

"Oh, I don't know," he says, pushing his chair back a few feet. "Shit, forget it!"

He sits staring at his hands for a while, and I wait in silence. The battered clock on the table ticks audibly.

Finally he blurts out in a rush, "Son-of-a-bitch! You know what my old man said to me this week?! I mean, he's really nowhere! Unbelievable!" He gestures roughly with one hand and says, "Wait a minute, wait a minute. Let me take it from the beginning."

He puts the ash tray back on the table and runs his hands through his shoulder-length hair. Then he rests his elbows on the arms of the chair and presses his knuckles against his temples.

"Like I said, I've been doing a lot of thinking about my parents lately. I don't know, something we said in here a couple of weeks ago got me going. And like, I was thinking to myself, here I am putting them down and calling them hypocrites with all their phony 1930s liberal bullshit about 'humanity' and crap, with their two cars and their TV and their imitation Japanese furniture and gold-tasseled shower curtains and electric toothbrushes—and then I thought, 'Shit, I'm doing the same thing!' Like here I am, playing Mr. Cool, making the 'in' scene, being hip and above it all, and meanwhile, I'm sponging off them and their money and just laying around putting everyone down."

Stan leans back in the chair and shakes his head as if to clear it of the thought.

He continues, "Well, that really freaked my head when I thought about it. I tried to come up with all kinds of excuses like, 'Since it all goes for shit anyway, what difference does it make?' and, 'This culture's gotta get worse before it gets better, so why the fuck not spend a little money and be happy?' But I just couldn't feel the same after that."

He pauses and takes off his glasses. His eyes are a startling, clear blue.

"So anyway, I kept thinking about them and decided it had been a long time since we'd last sat down and tried to talk to each other. So I get my ass together and take myself on a subway out to Queens. My old man opens the door and doesn't say a word. He just opens the door and goes back to his newspapers like I wasn't even there. My mother's watching some quiz program on TV. 'Hello, Stanley,' she says, 'There's some cold chicken in the icebox if you're hungry.' I stand in front of my old man and say, 'Hey, dad, can I talk to you for a minute?' And do you know what he says to me, that bastard? Without even looking up from his paper, he says, 'Go wash your face and comb that ridiculous hair first.' Can you believe that?!"

"So what did you do?"

"I said, 'Listen, you dumb clod, I'm your son, I'm a grown man, and I want to talk to you.' So my mother says, without looking up from her TV, 'Don't talk to your father like that.' So I just said, 'Oh, shit,' and left."

He crosses his long legs and glances at the clock.

"What night was this?"

"Tuesday."

"So then, the next night you thought you might just go out with some friends and do some acid. Funny coincidence."

"Yeah, I thought of that. And then I thought, shit, that would just be giving in to the bastard. He'd probably love it. He could go to work and play the martyr with his friends. Or he could call my sister in Detroit and do his whole number on her that starts with, 'Your crazy, good-for-nothing brother was here. . . .' "

He offers me a piece of gum. I take it and say, "You know, while you've been talking, it occurred to me that there's one pretty striking difference between you now and when you first came here."

"What's that?"

"One of the first things you said to me was, 'I have no feelings. I'm not like other people. I don't feel anything. Nothing is real. Once in a while when I smoke or take acid, things get beautiful and I feel good some of the time, but the rest is empty.' Do you remember that?"

He nods.

"Well," I continue, "you seem to have had some feelings today. Granted they weren't pleasant ones, but they were strong and not empty. And certainly not unreal. Feelings about your parents, and even before that, feelings about being in this crummy room."

"Yeah," he says, trying to sound tough, "so where does that get me?"

"Well, if you're allowing yourself to be aware of your feelings about things, that's a first step to knowing where you're at and what you want to do about it."

"Assuming I *want* to do something about it," he tacks on.

"That's right. That's a 'given.' Always assuming you want to do something about it. That's up to you."

He stands up abruptly and puts his glasses back on. "Yeah, well, I'll think about it. That's enough for today," he says, taking over. "My head's spinning, and I got some things to do. There's only a few minutes left, anyway. Okay with you?"

"It's your time, Stan. If you don't want to use the next ten minutes, that's up to you, too. If you'd like to get into it sometime, we could talk about why you might have decided to leave at this particular point in the session."

He stops at the door and thinks a minute. "Yeah, right. You think it might be *significant*, huh, doc?" he says, with a sarcastic emphasis on the word.

"Don't you?"

"Too much!" He collapses theatrically against the wall. As he straightens up and tucks in a flap of shirt, he says, "Yeah, sure. Right on! Next time, maybe . . . See ya next week."

"So long, Stan. See you then."

He bops out the door, looking cool.

With the extra ten minutes before Nancy's session, I tilt back the chair and gratefully close my eyes for a few seconds, thinking of nothing in particular, but vaguely pleased that Stan has been able to sustain this commitment to therapy.

Nancy presents a different kind of problem. Bright, quick, she has been punctual for her appointments, and, for the most part, has been superficially compliant in therapy. Nancy is an aspiring actress, and here, too, she has "played at" being a "good patient."

She came for treatment on her own, because of a repetitive laryngitis that "managed to crop up" at crucial times just prior to major auditions or performances. After a few weeks in therapy, she had been able to grasp some of the psychodynamic implications of the problem, and it had rather dramatically disappeared.

Her major investment since we started, however, has been to resist any attempt to reach a "feeling" level, though she has indulged in some almost convincing histrionic scenes, which have effectively shielded her from having to deal with genuine issues or interactions.

I let the chair down with a thud and buzz the secretary to send Nancy in.

"You know what I realized today?" Nancy says, taking off a black mohair jacket and dusting the seat with her hand before she sits down.

She is heavily made up this afternoon, with long false

lashes, a bright-red 1920s mouth, and a stylish tousled hairdo. Her Garbolike features have been cleverly accentuated with subtle shadings and highlights.

"What?" I ask.

"That I haven't had a cold, laryngitis, the flu, anything, since that dynamite session we had. Can you believe that! Wow! It seems like yesterday in some ways. But I feel light-years away from the poor little girl who came in here crying because she couldn't find her voice. Speaking of crying, I'd better not do any of that today. It took me an hour to do this face, and I have an appointment with a very important agent after I leave."

"Is this the one you've been trying to see for so long?"

"Don Savage. Yes. God, I just dread it, Judy!" She smoothes her long, charcoal-gray dress with nails the color of her lips. Then she looks up wide-eyed and asks timidly, "Could we get into it a little bit? I shouldn't be this scared. . . . Why are you smiling like that?"

"Your asking me in that tone of voice."

"What tone of—oh!" she blushes. "Maybe I'm not as far from that poor little girl as I thought," she says, "Gawd!"

She clears her throat comically, sits up straight in the chair, and says in a husky, deep voice, "Well now. I'd like to explore the question of my disproportionate anxiety in regard to this upcoming interview. Let's begin."

I make a gesture inviting her to begin.

She falls back into the chair and says, "Shit. I don't know where to start. Help."

I look at her blankly.

"Really, Judy! I can't think of a thing. My mind's an empty screen."

"Well," I offer, "what do you think will happen when you get there? What does it feel like?"

She closes her eyes. "I'll get there and even though I have an appointment for three thirty, like all agents, he'll keep me waiting for an hour or so. Then, when I finally get to

see him for my ten or fifteen minutes, I'll have to show him
my pictures, turn on all the charm, and convince him that
I'm the world's greatest actress—all so that he can decide
whether he will or won't deign to represent me. And nothing that we say will relate in any way to what's really going
on. It will all be one well-rehearsed, stupid game we'll be
playing. Ugh!"

"Does that remind you of anything?" I ask.

She opens her eyes, and says, "Does what remind me of
anything?"

"Selling yourself, putting on an act, to get something
from an important man?"

"Eeek!" She throws her arms over her head and says, "Of
course! Oh, god, I can't stand it! It's so fuckin' classical!
Back to good ole daddy again. Over and over and over and
OVER!"

Nancy's father had been a Hungarian refugee who had
made his own way through a new language and culture to
become a successful businessman in import-export. He'd
met his wife through a mutual friend, and after a short,
formal courtship, he had married this pious, silent woman,
who'd been taught to expect nothing more from life than
to serve a husband, bring up children, and worship God.

The couple had had two children: Jerry, their first-born,
and Nancy, who had been a rebel almost from the beginning. To retain some kind of integrity, Nancy had learned
quickly how to manipulate her parents, playing at being a
model child and skillfully doing pretty much as she
pleased.

Though for weeks she had talked about her "perfect
family" in sessions with me, it had gradually become painfully obvious to us both that there had never been any real
exchange of affection, except at times between her and
Jerry, with whom she would share confidences, giggle and
laugh conspiratorially, or sometimes pout and fight, usually about his special privileges as a boy. Jerry was in fact

allowed more personal freedom, but he and Nancy had an unstated alliance against their parents, and would often cover for each other.

At an early age, Nancy had abandoned efforts to make significant contact with her mother. The woman was uncomplaining, unimaginative, and unavailable, except to feed and clothe her children and cushion them through bruised knees, measles, and sore throats. For serious problems, Nancy turned to her dynamic, restless father, who listened only if her questions corresponded with his conception of what was appropriate for a nice girl to be thinking about.

Nancy gets up and paces around the room, rehashing memories of being cute and seductive for special attention and favors from him. Her father tended to ignore her otherwise.

" 'Going through a phase' was his favorite expression. 'It will pass, you'll get over it, you'll see. Now run along.' But do my whole cutsie number, and he'd say, 'Now, that's my girl! Come give us a kiss.' Oh, god, it's right out of a fuckin' textbook! I can't believe it really happened."

She sits down again and stares into space.

"It's funny," she says distractedly, "how much I talk about him and almost never about my mother. She was always so gentle and saintly and passive, cooking, cleaning, tucking me and Jerry in, never complaining, never saying much of anything, come to think of it. She had her religion. I guess that was where most of her emotions went. Her parents were strict Lutherans. My grandfather was like a man of stone. But it's strange. I have a feeling that in her own way, my mother reinforced all my craziness. I can't think how, really, but it feels true. She almost never got upset. I could probably count on my fingers the number of times she did. Oh, my god—"

Nancy's face registers surprise.

"What is it?" I ask.

She answers with a kind of amazement, "I just remembered something that I haven't thought of since it happened. It was one of those few times my mother got upset. I'm not sure what it has to do with all this, but Jesus, I was so embarrassed at the time. It's so vivid, I can even remember the fixtures in the bathroom. They were white porcelain and had the manufacturer's name baked into the glaze, but I was too young to read yet, so I used to pretend it was a magic word you could wish on when you touched it in a special way."

She pauses with the recollection.

"Anyway," she continues, "I was really little. I couldn't even reach up to the shower handles. I'd been playing my magic game in the bathtub, and my mother came in to take me out and dry me. She noticed this black-and-blue mark or bruise or something on the inside of one of my thighs and got really upset. I don't know where I got it. Playing outdoors probably. I was a real tomboy. Well, she started yelling at me to tell her what had happened. I couldn't understand some of the things she said, but there was something about had I let any boys touch me there and it was dirty and I had to learn to be a good girl always or I would never grow up and find a nice husband. Well, I was pretty young at the time, and I just remember feeling very confused and embarrassed like I'd done something wrong, but I didn't know what. I must have looked pretty bewildered, because she suddenly stopped talking and looked embarrassed herself. I asked her what was wrong and she said, 'Nothing. Never mind. Let's get you into your pajamas now and we'll go read a story.' "

Nancy stops, still lost in the memory. She sits thoughtfully, regarding the clock, chin in hand.

I wait a few moments, then summarize. "So you have a father who rewards you for being a shallow, pretty little girl who acts brainless and one-dimensional, and a mother who's the stereotype of the good housewife and who manages to make you feel guilty about your sexuality from as far back as you can remember. And until very recently, a culture that strongly reinforced all those messages from your parents."

Nancy looks up and says lightly, "Yeah. Pretty fucked, huh? No wonder I can never tell when I'm acting and when I'm being real."

As an afterthought, she adds, "And then I go and marry a man for a year who shows me off at all the best clubs and treats me like shit the rest of the time. Christ, like I said, no wonder. No wonder I'm an actress. I come by it naturally, for pete's sake!"

She looks over at me and asks, "Wow, we gotta lot of work to do, don't we?"

"Nothing you can't resolve in a reasonable amount of time," I reassure her. "You've got a good head on your shoulders."

"I have?" she says, startled. "Nobody ever told me that before. At home, my brother was supposed to be the smart one, the one my parents had to save money for to send to college. They said it would be a waste of time for me."

"I know. You have lots of company with that one," I tell her.

Nancy's remark reminds me of a garage mechanic when I was in junior high school. He laughed at my parents when they told him I wanted to be a doctor. Winding up the gasoline pump, he sneered over his stump of a cigar, "What a joke! She'll be married with two kids by the time she's twenty-one. Don't make me laugh!"

Nancy looks troubled and asks, "Does the fact that I'm beginning to get some clues about what makes me tick and why I chose the career I did make the acting profession a bunch of crap?"

I remember a similar set of fears when I began my own therapy. When it became clear to me that I'd grown used to "parenting" my own parents through their drunken hazes and chronic illnesses, it was no mystery why I'd chosen a profession for myself that involved caring for other people. My first impulse after making the connection had been to run from it. To accept that I also enjoyed my work for other reasons and that I had some real talent for it took a little longer.

"Not at all," I answer. "You know from the feedback you've gotten in your classes and from the summer-stock reviews that you're considered a sensitive and talented performer. Why should any insight you gain negate your ability? If anything, I should think it would give you a greater depth."

She brightens. "I could use a little of that!"

I glance at the clock. "It's time, Nancy."

"Right," she says, pulling on the mohair jacket.

I wish her good luck with the agent.

"Thanks, I'll need it. But I feel a lot better now about the interview. Double thanks."

She leaves, trailing a strong scent of rose that recalls a rose-scented hand lotion one of the matrons in the Dublin obstetrics hospital used to apply between clinics.

Strange, brittle-looking, gray-haired woman with heavy dark brows that nearly met across her forehead. She would stand prim and efficient in her starched, spotless-white apron and blue uniform behind the white-coated physicians, hands clasped in front of her, ready to do their bidding. During breaks, she would shoo the timid student nurses into a corner to lecture them about the correct way to set up an examining tray. Occasionally, for reasons that were never clear to me, a young nurse would be dismissed from the group and disappear down the corridor, eyes brimming with tears of rebellion. The matron would return to her discourse, tight-lipped and seemingly unmoved. The fragrant hand lotion never left the pocket of her uniform. I could never reconcile it; it seemed so out of character.

At a clinic one day, an exhausted-looking woman in her early thirties was told she might be pregnant for the ninth time. When the doctors had left, the woman lay back and burst into tears, her feet still up in the stirrups.

"Stop your foolishness now!" the matron had snapped. "Get dressed and behave yourself. You're acting like a two-year-old! For shame, for shame!"

A pale, silent nurse helped the woman off the examining table. The woman pleaded, "Sister, please, isn't there something we could do about it? It's been one a year almost. Do you know what that's like? Please, anything!"

The young nurse and I were looking at the matron from a respectable distance. The woman had begun to put on a patched and shabby dress as she waited for a reply. Matron washed her hands and pulled the pink lotion from her pocket.

"What do you expect me to do?" she said, as the cubicle filled with the scent of roses. "If you want to stop having babies, you know what you and your husband can do about it."

As the woman dried her eyes with the back of her hand, the matron walked away, already oblivious and disinterested, massaging her fingers and palms.

The cats come to greet me, sniffing at the snow on my shoes, but I can see no sign of John in the quiet apartment. The door to the bathroom is ajar. I push it open farther, to be warmed by a rush of moist, spicy air.

John's head is wreathed by a mountain of fragrant bubbles. He opens his eyes and smiles. "Hello, love! Come on in, the water's fine! Great fun lying here watching your American snow come down behind yon African violet in the window!"

I kiss him hello and he encircles my neck with a dripping bubble-arm.

"God, this is like being enveloped by the abominable snowman! Let go of me and let me get out of my clothes!"

"A minor detail, but a good point. Not absolutely necessary, but convenient. Yes, do that, please. Oh, but darling," he says, affecting a heavy British accent, "before you begin to disrobe, do kindly fetch me another glass of this superb wine I found, will you? Lovely ruby color!"

He produces a large, empty goblet from the depths of his blanket of bubbles.

"Good lord! A naked, drunken Irishman in my bathtub! What else do you have under there? Not a smoked salmon by any chance?"

John secretively parts the bubbles and peers down into the hollow he has created. "No, no salmon here. But something much more meaty and delicious, if you'd care to come in and sample it!"

I sit on the edge of the tub.

John responds by quickly pulling the bubbles back over the space. "Halt, halt! No previews! If you're joining this feast, kindly get into the proper attire for it."

"What? Not even an appetizer? Stingy, aren't you?"

"Well, this is highly irregular, but never let it be said . . ."

He sloshes to his feet in the water, proudly displaying his soap-bedecked erection and striking a dignified pose.

"Fanfares only, please, no vulgar applause," he says to Sam and Clyde staring at him from the doorway. Seemingly taken unawares, he shouts, "Wait! Help! Woman on the loose! Be careful, Judith, you'll drown! Ah-h-h, you've the mouth and tongue of a genius, an absolute genius!"

He takes the goblet from my hand, puts it in the sink, leans closer against me, says, "Oh, my god, I can't stand it! To hell with the wine! Come here, you dissolute woman," and starts to pull me into the bath.

"John, my clothes!"

"Yes, well," he counters, letting go, "you started this, you know! All right, I'll try to be civilized for a maximum of five minutes, but that's all, you understand!"

Pouting, he relents and flops heavily back in the water.

I retrieve the glass from the sink and go in search of the open wine bottle.

"While you're in there, love," he calls after me, "you might slice us each a bit of fish on a plate."

"You have to be kidding!"

"Not at all. On the contrary. After all, it's a small enough request," he muses. "A little salmon, a little sex, a little salmon, a little sex, a little—"

"All right, all right, already!" I interrupt. "I get the idea! Hang on there a minute, will you?" I find a tray large enough to fit across the tub and take the salmon from the top shelf of the refrigerator.

"Oh, I'm hanging on, all right," he chimes, and sings a stanza from an obscene Irish song about masturbation.

Having set out the food and wine, I unbutton my dress in the kitchen near the heater. I watch the pine logs burning in the fireplace in the next room and notice that the floor nearby is comfortably littered with pillows, books, newspapers, and a collection of various house plants. Feeling suddenly tender and moved, I carry in the tray and deposit it across the bathtub.

John interrupts his song to say, "We have a serious problem to solve. I've been trying to figure out a way to eat you and the salmon at the same time. Think we can work that out?"

He sees my expression and his face changes.

"Is anything wrong, Judith?" he asks in concern, reaching a wet arm out to me.

"No. No, nothing, darling," I reassure him, kissing the palm of his hand. "I just love you very much."

He takes my wrist and draws me into the water, watching my eyes and saying softly, "Come in and get warm and have some lovely wine with me. My dear, darling creature. Poor, deluded, head-doctor. What on earth have you done getting mixed up with the likes of me?"

We sit opposite each other across the tray, staring, taking

wine, saying nothing. We feed each other fish and imported cheeses. The cats come to share the meal. John fixes them a plate of the leftovers and puts the tray on the floor. We sip our wine and watch them eat. My lover's hand is smooth and warm between my thighs. We inflame each other slowly with soap and handfuls of bath oil, and then we make love in the water with a growing intensity that frightens the cats from the room. Then we dry our oiled bodies, bring our glasses of wine to the fire and we make love again on a mattress on the floor. Afterward, we lie quietly watching the logs burn.

"John?"

"Yes, love."

"Not now necessarily, but sometime by the end of my training, do you think we could think about having a child?"

He rolls over on his back and regards me seriously.

"Judith. There's nothing that would give me more plea-sure than to have a child with you. But you know my situation—"

"Yes, I know. And I wouldn't expect you to leave your work or family. But I've given it a lot of thought, and I'd like to have one anyway. At least one."

"Have you really considered thoroughly what you're saying? It's difficult enough for two people to raise chil-dren, but a woman alone . . ."

He thinks for a minute and adds, "Of course, there's always the possibility that you may meet someone you'll want to live with, but what if it doesn't happen?"

"I've really thought it through, John. Over and over. And I'm sure I could manage without much trouble. My profession should bring me enough of an income to hire adequate help. I could move to a larger place and have a housekeeper live in, that kind of thing."

I sit up and take his hand and go on. "I'm past thirty now, and it's an experience I'd like not to miss in life, John. I don't know if I'll find another conventional relationship again or not. But I can't and don't particularly want to wait much longer to find out."

John sits up also. He stares deeply into the fire and asks, "Have you talked to Dr. Bernstein about this yet?"

"Yes, many times. He said, 'Why not? Just make sure you can afford them.' "

John grimaces and says, "Have either of you considered that it might be nice for a child to have a father? I'm sorry, Judith, I don't mean to sound sarcastic, but it does seem rather important to me."

"Yes, Dr. Bernstein and I have talked about it. And of course, it would be better. But John, not to disparage them, I spend a major part of my day working with people who are casualties from conventional 'nuclear families.' And by the same token, there have been all throughout history, and there are today, any number of happy outcomes from improbable or atypical situations. Just look around..."

I try to tone down my earnestness and add in a softer tone of voice, "I think our child, or children, would have just as good a break as any. They'd be wanted and loved. And that's more than a fighting chance to begin with."

John throws another log on the fire and pokes around at the coals with a large piece of wood. Then, replacing the screen, he says to me rather sadly, "Selfishly, Judith, I suppose what bothers me most about it is that I wouldn't be here with you to share it all. It's truly wondrous, having a child and watch it grow. And *your* child—"

He looks at me for a long moment, caresses my head, and says, "God, I think I'd want to be here every minute! I don't know that I could bear it, darling."

Sam curls himself into a ball in my lap. The room is rosy from the fire. I stroke the cat and persist, "But, despite the pain of separation, which we experience anyway, wouldn't it be better to have a child than not to? And we could still continue to meet as we have been."

John sighs, "And suppose you find someone you want to live with?"

"Then we'll all try to work it out together."

He looks over at me open-mouthed, and I say quickly, "I'll never stop loving you, no matter who I meet. He'd have to know about you beforehand, and we'd have to see what we could work out. John, I can't predict how you or I or anyone else will react in a situation that hasn't occurred, that's only a fantasy."

John laughs hollowly. The muscles of his jaw work silently, and he asks with a certain harshness, "Do you really think you'd ever meet a man who'd be willing to share you?"

I feel my face flush with anger. "John, you're talking about me like some possession, even *you* are treating me like an object, as though all we've known and shared with each other were irrelevant to what we've been saying! And it's not, damn it! And I know you don't really think about me that way. I think you trust my integrity and my feeling for you, and I've always believed you would be open and tolerant of my struggles with my own loneliness."

He gives me a friendly push, and Sam yawns and looks for a quieter place to sleep.

John says, "Of course I trust your integrity, you mutt! And, of course, I'd try to be tolerant. It would hurt, though."

I touch his face. We look at each other silently, and I find myself feeling the volumes of information that are communicated without a word. Maybe it would be better just to shut up. I don't.

"Of course, it would hurt," I continue softly. "It would be impossible to grow up in this culture and have it not hurt. But I think we'd survive. We seem to have survived everything else so far, without causing each other or anyone else too much pain."

John draws me closer to his side and puts his arm around me.

"Yes," he says, "Yes, I think that's true. But do you really think you'll easily meet anyone else with tolerance enough for some kind of . . . 'arrangement'?"

"I don't think I'll *easily* meet anyone, but not because I think there's a lack of tolerance for 'unconventional' relationships. I really believe in people, in their potential for understanding and flexibility, in civilization. And I think that there are all kinds of things happening, good things that will add to our culture, that have added already, in fact. No. If I fail to meet anyone else, and I have for several years, as you may have noticed"—I kiss him and whisper in his ear—"if I fail to meet anyone else, it's because, so to speak, everyone compared to you is such an anticlimax!"

He collapses spread-eagle on the floor.

"I give up!" he groans, staring at the ceiling for divine intervention, "You crazy, mixed-up psychiatrist! God help your poor unsuspecting patients!"

Then he turns his head and looks at me hopefully, asking, "Do I at least get a dinner out of this ordeal?"

"What would you like, you insatiable beast?! There's a refrigerator full of food."

"Meat! Steak! Thick, juicy steak!"

"Coming up, milord."

I moan exaggeratedly to my feet, search through the closet, and pull on a floor-length Indian housedress the color of cornflowers. My body smells of sex and sandalwood bath oil.

On the way to the kitchen, John calls, "Judith."

"Yes, love?"

"We'll think about the child for a while and talk again, shall we? I'm basically for it, you know."

"Okay, yes, I know."

"I know it's not quite the same kind of creativity, but meanwhile, you have the book."

"That's true, John. Meanwhile, there's the book."

Peeling some potatoes and onions, I reflect on John's seemingly endless capacity to absorb, assimilate, and respond to all kinds of people and situations with a something that is creative, forceful, and genuinely loving and compassionate. An intuitiveness and a kind of animal energy that—

A kiss on the back of my neck interrupts my train of thought.

"I want you to know something, woman."

"What's that?"

"You're a force. A willful, undisciplined, difficult creature, but a force. Remember that."

"Funny. I was just thinking something very close to that about you."

He retreats into humor. "Fine. Well, now that we've patted each other on the back, I'll go and have my pee. You cook, please."

I vaguely wonder where I might be if I had not had the experience of a relationship with this man. I have long ago abandoned attempts to define or analyze it further than a thing we mutually share which does not seem to lose its energy or availability for expansion.

The translucent slices of potato and onion spatter in the oil. I unwrap a thick porterhouse steak and ready it for the broiler. Somewhere in the crisper are the ingredients for a spinach salad.

It occurs to me that I am deeply grateful that Ben and I had the strength to end a ten-year marriage that was beginning to devour us both for reasons that had only partly to do with our individual claims on craziness. We were also caught in a cliché.

There were the usual Hollywood movie and television metaphors into which we had been born and brought up. Despite Ben's philosophical sophistication and existential predilection, there was the hidden double-standard, where

it was to be understood that none of his "casual encoun-
ters" with women "really meant" anything, but I must be
careful not to seem too friendly with a waiter or friends
who came to the house. There were the American middle-
class mind games, with their pseudo-psychiatric jargon and
psychological half-truths, which systematically under-
mined any possibility for a real understanding of what we
may have been feeling and subtly destroyed our potential
for gentleness and compassion with each other.

And there was the competition. We had been determined
not to let it get to us, but at some pretty crucial moments
in our relationship it did, and we could not afford another
divisive force. From the beginning, its flames were fostered
and fanned along the way by unthinking or openly malevolent people. . . .

*A fat, loud-mouthed relative of Ben's stuffing his mouth with
corned beef and assessing me like a piece of horseflesh: "I don't
understand that Bennie," he finally decides, "he used to have the
nicest girls in the neighborhood at his feet. No insult intended, but
a couple of 'em had these gorgeous boobs. You got a nice ass, though.
But I wonder, why'd he decide to pick you in the end?"*

*The vivid memory of paunchy Dean Kott, the pre-medical guid-
ance counselor at NYU, trying to discourage Ben from medical
school. After being graduated from high school at fifteen and sweep-
ing through a year at Iowa State University with straight As, Ben
had grown bored. He'd taken off and hitchhiked across the country,
getting odd jobs with traveling circuses or working hat stands with
his uncles at country fairs. Then he'd come back to New York City
and made some close friends in Greenwich Village. At some point,
he'd decided to return to college and get a degree in philosophy or
history. We met in our junior year at NYU, when I had all but
discarded plans for medicine after the agonizing tedium of two
semesters of inorganic chemistry and easy honors in all my arts
courses. Ben had given up on grades, studied only when he felt like*

it, and toyed with dropping the whole thing again. After a deliri-
ously happy spring and summer together, we stayed up late one
night talking, over my now-ancient, snoring Labrador retriever.
I remembered some of my original reasons for wanting to go into
medicine and couldn't think of viable alternatives. At about 4:00
A.M., *I decided to re-register for the pre-med program and finish*
the requirements. Ben had been listening carefully to my arguments
with myself and said simply, "You know, that sounds like a good
idea, Jude. Think I might just give it a try."

Together we'd gone to Dean Kott for advice and suggestions. He
was an arch-conservative World War II veteran whom the students
had descriptively named Fart-Waddle.

"Why, you're not much better than a common bum, are you,
Ben? Look at you, for God's sake! What are you, a hippie or
something? How do you expect to get into med school with these
marks? Ridiculous! Out of the question," he'd drawled in his south-
ern bass, shaking his head and farting. "Why, look at your wife's
record now! Dean's List every semester!"

In a different, oily tone, he'd added, "How did you ever get a
pretty little girl like this to marry you, anyway? She needs a real
man who can supply her with everything her little heart desires, so
she'll give up her foolishness about becoming a doctor."

Then he'd grunted to himself and concluded, "Huh! Well, that's
all I have to say. In short, forget it, friend. You haven't got a
chance."

The med school interviewers had agreed with Fart-Waddle.
None of them had even seriously considered Ben. They had a little
more difficulty with me because of my consistently high grades and
honors. With each of the fourteen applications apiece that we'd
filed, we'd had to send a ten-dollar fee, taken from student loans,
summer savings, and relatives. The fee was supposedly to cover the
cost of application review and an interview, if one was granted,
which more often than not it wasn't. As rejection after rejection
was added to the official pile on our desk, we began to think about
applying overseas. Ben's mother's boss was said to have "pull" in
the British Isles. Though it was patently absurd to do so, we

*doggedly went to the remaining American interviews. One of the
last interviewers at least had a little more honesty, or perhaps it
was a little less discretion, in concluding his talk with me.*

*"Look, do I have to draw you a picture, lady?" The pasty-faced
doctor had leaned back in his chair, saying, "Phi Beta Kappa,
Dean's List scholar notwithstanding, statistically you'll be pregnant by your sophomore year in medical school. We can't afford the
investment. Nice grades, but sorry."*

To Ben he had said simply, "You just haven't got what it takes."

*Of the fourteen places to which we had applied, one of the newer,
more fashionable institutions which did not want to be accused of
sexual discrimination accepted me. Ben was out of luck. We decided
to leave the country.*

*With the help of my mother-in-law's boss, we got into the best-
known medical school in Ireland. The university to which it belonged had been established by Queen Elizabeth I. It had a long
liberal academic tradition and the only library in the country
where the extremely rigid book ban did not apply at the time.
Tragicomically, it was the only place you could find a copy of
Joyce's* Ulysses *then. It was a den of iniquity in the middle of the
capital city. Some of our Catholic classmates had had to request
special dispensations from the archbishop to attend.*

*In medical school, Ben discovered a calling, easily mastered even
the most difficult material, and was looked on as a kind of eccentric
genius. We were both in the top 5 percent of our class. It went
smoothly enough in the beginning, but during the five-year program, an insidious male-female power struggle got set up that was
aided by examiners and fellow classmates.*

*After one Saturday morning "spot" exam, Ben sat and berated
himself for an hour about the questions he had missed. He'd scored
three points lower than I that day. Our marks were 98 and 95.*

*But it was usually the other way around, and since that was
considered the "natural order" of things, there was no overt discomfort or outcry most of the time. The possibilities for sadistic enjoyment of the situation were, however, multiple.*

On an end-of-the-year final, one British examiner had smiled down his long aristocratic nose and said, "Forgive us for taking you after your husband, madam, but you do follow him in the alphabet. Tell me, are you as intelligent as he? We understand he's at the top of your class, and I must say, he's done very well indeed on the questions we've just put to him. Well, we'll know the answer soon, won't we? Would you kindly care to describe for us the effects of a lesion on the nucleus of the third cranial nerve?"

Not long afterward, when we were celebrating the end of the exam month, some drunken classmate shouted across the pub, "Who wears the pants in that family, anyway? You ought to be home having kids and doing the laundry. You're built to have kids, you know." And he had come over and punctuated his remarks with a lascivious slap on the rear.

Ben walked off with nearly all the prizes in our class and a good deal of resentment from his closest competitors.

After our first year, I had withdrawn from the contest and been reasonably satisfied to graduate with honors in medicine. I suppose I should qualify the "reasonably satisfied." The phrase is loaded and has a history:

Our second year of medical school had been particularly trying for me. During a three-week vacation on the Continent, Ben had begun an affair with a German woman, which continued by mail after our return to Ireland. It was especially bad timing, for we had been feeling unusually close and in touch prior to the trip.

When we'd returned to classes, Ben had kept insisting the thing was over and had meant nothing. Carelessly, he left a few compromising letters around the house. I read them. And later (with my marks in school suffering and my self-respect generally deteriorating) I began to search his clothes and belongings for more evidence, hating my sneakiness and intrusion on his privacy, but doing it anyway. The situation came to a head one evening when I flew across the living room and started attacking him like an animal. He simply held me away until I started to cry.

After that, I sat down and thought to myself, "Nobody, not Ben, and especially not I, should allow myself to disintegrate to this degree. There have to be alternatives. . . ."

It occurred to me that what had been perhaps most destructive had been the lack of dialogue during the four- or five-month period. Ben had continually and earnestly denied that anything was going on, and I kept believing him. Then I would discover more letters and wonder where he'd really gone for weekends. But beyond accusations and denials, we hadn't talked.

My animal attack had sobered me. I was supposed to love this man. If that was true, I should be able to discuss with him how I felt and then care enough about him to let him do what he felt he had to do.

After washing my face and swallowing my embarrassment, I apologized for my assault and made it clear that although I was hurting, I would make no further attempts to interfere. Ben expressed his gratitude and told me that he wanted to go to Germany for a week. I nodded and asked when he was planning to leave.

"I'd like to go this weekend," he said, then hesitated and asked with concern, "Will you be here when I get back?"

"I don't know. I'll have to see what happens, how I feel. I'll try to be. That's the most I can say."

I felt strangely quiet inside and was relieved to have remembered my sense of dignity and reason. Ben left for the airport Saturday morning at nine. He was back in half an hour.

"I must be out of my head," he said simply, "I want to be here."

During the whole period, our classmates and teachers had wondered about my worsening performance on exams. At a cocktail party one evening, an especially malevolent professor had said to me, "I always knew Ben would win out in the end. He has a real scientific mind. Takes no effort for him. You just struggle along well sometimes. Knew I was right."

That, plus constant questions from my classmates, some of them genuinely concerned about what had happened, nearly finished off my self-esteem. Later, when I'd regained a sense of proportion and begun to take an interest in my work again, I developed a rich loathing for the emphasis on competitiveness and grades with which I'd grown up and had accepted unquestioningly. I resolved to try to enjoy the work for itself and retain what I thought was vital to my future practice. But even if it had to be a conscious act of will on my part, I was going to give up on the one-upmanship, the trying to second-guess the professors before exams, the anxiety about one or two points.

Ben had continued at the top of the class through the whole affair and stayed there, with incredible facility, for the rest of our time in med school. One of the prizes he'd won in the third year was a partial scholarship. He was required to attend a formal dinner for the presentation. It was the party season, and the day of the dinner we ran all over Dublin trying in vain to find a rented tuxedo that would fit him. He finally had to settle for a suit two sizes too large, and we were on our way home in the late afternoon when we ran into a group of men in our class who insisted on taking him for a drink to celebrate. I took the tuxedo home to press, with a firm promise from Ben that he'd be home in an hour to change. The dinner was at 8.00 P.M., and he came reeling in the door a little after half past seven. I threw him into a hot tub, gave him a large cup of coffee and two aspirin, and helped him climb into the tux. The waist was so wide, it made him look like Emmet Kelly. I found two large safety pins and fixed the pants to his shirt to keep them from falling down. He grinned crookedly and lurched out the door.

The dinner will probably never be forgotten. It was held in the provost's mansion. Ben fell in love with a portrait of some British soldier whom he insisted was Cornwallis. Apparently, he had waxed with drunken eloquence to a scandalized audience about how "we really beat the shit out of that guy in 1781. Nice guy, though. . . ."

They had served three different wines with the dinner, and brandy after dessert. Finally, when Ben was no longer able to stand, some magnanimous soul had offered to drive him home. He was deposited at the door, scholarship certificate in hand. After I managed to get him undressed, he murmured something close to "great party—of all people, guess who was there? . . . Would you believe Cornwallis? . . ." and fell asleep.

It was one of the few times during the five-year period of training that we remembered our sense of humor.

*When we returned to the States, Ben was greeted like the con-
quering hero. He met the flattery of awestruck nurses and a wide-
eyed flower-child overwhelmed with the vision of the hip, handsome
doctor. Nice, good-looking girls again, who "would have done
anything" for him. Full circle.*

*In the last two years of our marriage, there was a gradual
falling off of dialogue, a mutual mind-fucking, a final breach in
trust and communication. A week after an especially vicious exchange, I moved into a furnitureless apartment with the cats and
the multicolored shell of a sea urchin to recapture a sense of privacy
and dimension.*

*Ben was hurt and enraged, and, for a while, uncharacteristically
selfish. We had a separation agreement that read, "All possessions,
personal belongings, including car . . . shall be the exclusive property of the husband."*

*But then, through our distance, we began to share again, only
tentatively at first.*

Numb. Healing.

*A few months later, a pained telephone call from Ben acknowl-
edged the jointness of our despair and self-deception.*

"Can I help, Judy?"

"I don't know."

"Neither do I. But you know I'm here if you need me."

"Likewise."

"How are you?"

"Better. And you?"

"Better."

"Let's stay in touch."

"Yes, I'd like to."

"Well, take care."

"You, too."

I'd met John in the pub about a year before Ben and I
returned to the States. Somehow this gentle, marvelous
administrator-poet had read the bleeding rawness in my

eyes and answered with his own. He had loved me. He had known a lot. He had encouraged me to go on in medical school. He had urged me to stay in my marriage and try to work things out, reminding me that ten years was a considerable length of time to have lived with the same person and ought to be worthy of at least one last, sustained rescue effort. He could not have known that it was already too late. We didn't even know that. But by then, Ben and I had succumbed to the dictates of our own hangups and begun to suffocate within the boundaries of the context in which we found ourselves.

Mel Bernstein had helped me through the worst periods: the thinking about separation after Ben had refused to participate in couple therapy, the actual moving-out period, the aftermath of loneliness, quiet, a sense of personal failure and fatigue.

John calls, "Table's set. Anything else I can do?"
"No, love. The steak's almost ready. Just sit down and relax."

There were other phone calls and visits between Ben and me in the months after I moved out, and we had gradually recalled some of our original affection for each other. Something about the nature of time and circumstance spoke to the finality of the separation, but despite the loss, something vital had been spared and a significant kind of contact preserved. There was also a relief that we had not surrendered to the mutual, groveling deterioration that seemed to have overtaken so many generations of couples in Western society to a point of endless, robotlike, going-through-motions, punctuated by occasional outbursts of anger and frustration at the predicament.

John starts banging on the table with his silverware. "Food! Food and drink! Food!"

"Okay, okay! It's coming! Why don't you come help bring it in?"

"Delighted! As long as it gets me fed," he says, coming in from the other room.

Until I start eating, I do not realize how hungry I have become. We share our meal in relative silence, touching each other occasionally, fighting in furious pantomime over a piece of steak on the platter, feeding each other from our plates. We are down to bone and gristle when the phone intrudes on our privacy. As usual, I have a quick inner struggle about whether to answer it, and, as usual, end up catching it on the third ring.

Someone is shrieking unintelligibly on the other end, and after holding the receiver away from my ear for several seconds, I manage to get it across to the caller that I can't understand a word.

"Sorry, I'm just so excited! It's me, Clara!"

"What the hell has gotten into you?" I ask, remembering that she's working a double shift today.

"Didn't you hear me? She's eating! Beth's eating, you dumb doctor!" she screams.

"What? Beth! Clara, for real? What's she eating?" I wonder, as though it made any difference.

"Lamb chop, baked potato, and string beans!"

After a shocked silence, I hear Clara say, "Hello? Are you still there? Come in, please. Testing one, two, three. . . ."

I manage, "Did she say anything, Clara?"

"Only one thing, then she clammed up again. I went to her room to tell her supper was up, and she said, and I quote, 'Tell Judy Benetar, that's my doctor, that I don't want to go to a state hospital.' Then she put on a hospital bathrobe, walked into the day room, and helped herself to a plate of food. She's still in there. I just had to run and call you. Gotta go back now."

"Okay. Thanks so much, Clara!"

"Thought you'd get a boost outa that. Bye now, lovey!"

I hang up and turn around to see John wearing his over-coat walking out the door.

"John, where are you going?"

"Be right back." He winks and closes the door.

Perplexed, I shrug my shoulders and begin to collect the dishes, too flooded with feelings about the phone call to sort them all out. I let the hot water run on the plates while I open a new can of coffee. The fresh, strong odor that escapes the vacuum seems unusually precious at this moment. I scoop the grounds into the perc, plug it in, and turn to the dishes.

God, Beth came through! Beth's wonderful! I'm wonderful! People are wonderful! Maybe some of that stuff that I want to believe about autonomy is really true!

I reach under the sink for more liquid soap, wondering what had been going through Beth's head after I left.

Where to go next with her? Let her make the first move and try to meet her halfway if I can? For one thing, I have to be careful not to make too much of her eating or it will seem like condescension and will underline the power-struggle elements of the relationship. Wait to see if she says anything, and if not, maybe comment on what she said to Clara. Musn't get too planned about this. Leave room for spontaneity. And if—

John returns, nose and cheeks scarlet with cold, with a paper bag under his arm. He hangs up his coat, turns off the faucet, takes a towel and dries my hands, and leads me back to the fireside. He lights every candle in the room without a word, disappears, and reappears with his hands behind his back. His solemnity collapses, and, grinning from ear to ear, he produces a frosty bottle of champagne and two glasses.

"Ta-dah!" he trumpets through his hand, "Congratulations to you and Beth! I'm sorry she can't be here to join us!"

Then he lifts up my chin and says, "What are you crying for, silly?"

"I don't know. I'm just moved. Thank you, John."

He opens the champagne with dexterity, and the cork goes flying across the room. Clyde goes leaping after it. John fills our glasses carefully and hands me one. We stare at each other for a long moment.

"To you," he says.

"To you," I answer.

"And to Beth," he says.

The cats carouse with the cork.

"And to Sam and Clyde," I say.

"And to Mel Bernstein," he says.

"And to your work," I say.

"And yours," he says.

"And to autonomy," I say.

"Who's he?" he asks.

"A friend of ours," I say.

"Okay, I'll buy that," he says. Then he smiles and adds, "And to the salmon!"

"God yes, the salmon!" I say. "How could we leave that out?"

"And to love and sex!" he says.

"To all of us hungries," I say.

"Us who?" he asks.

"Hungries. Aren't we all 'hungry' in one way or another to different degrees?"

"Yes, I'd say so; and right now, I'm really getting hungry for some of this champagne!"

John does a little dance and raises his glass.

"To all of us, to love and sex and the salmon!" he says.

"To all of us, to love and sex and the salmon!" I repeat.

We clink and drain our glasses and then get gloriously drunk.

The snow on the side of the expressway is blackened with a week's accumulated city filth. Traffic has slowed to a crawl. There is a dull, dirty drizzle that nearly defeats the windshield wipers of my aunt's car. The radio plays some mediocre rock. I take my hand off the wheel and snap it off abruptly.

"What is it, Judith?" John asks.

"I hate it."

"What? The music, the traffic, driving to the airport?"

"I hate your leaving. I hate it."

"But you understand that—"

I cut him off. "Of course, I understand! Fuck understanding! I'm just trying to tell you how I *feel now,* and I feel terrible, hurt, enraged, abandoned. I go through this every bloody time, John. You come and open me up and I get to feeling all soft and vulnerable and warm and in touch with myself, and I just get to the point of real relaxing, a sense of peace and evenness and strength and courage, and wham! You disappear again. I hate it! I'm tired of being the one who 'understands.' Why can't someone else understand for a change? Why can't that uptight, narrow-minded, respectable society you live in try to understand something, before it withers up and atrophies completely like some desiccated turd? Why can't your delicate, sensitive wife understand, before someone, including her maybe, gets suffocated by her prim fragility? Why can't *you* understand, for pete's sake? Why do you have to be so goddamn protective of everyone—except me, of course, because I'll 'understand,' and that takes care of everything. Who told you to be everyone's hero and provider, anyway? Who the hell do you think you are, God or something?"

We drive in complete silence for the next half hour. I find it difficult to see through the tears flooding my eyes and running down my face onto my lap. In the parking lot at Kennedy, I turn off the motor and start to get out of the car.

John puts his hand on my arm, pulls me back in, and closes
and locks the door.

"Judith."

"What."

"Blow your nose."

He waits until I have found a tissue, dried my eyes and
nose, and looked up at him.

He says, "Judith. Thank you for reminding me we're
human."

"You're welcome," I say emptily, feeling suddenly
drained of energy.

John draws a breath and says, "I want to say something
else, but it's difficult to know how to put it. . . . I want to
be with you. I will try to be with you, somehow. The
'somehow' is the hard part. I don't know what we will work
out. Perhaps we'll have to go on with this arrangement.
Perhaps we'll find a better one. I don't know. I know that
I have a sense of movement, a feeling of growing intensity
and imbalance. I know that I want things for you, I want
things for myself, I want things for us. But whatever we try
to work out, it is absolutely vital to remember that there are
other people involved. And whatever we do we will do in
a civilized manner, by which I mean that we will do it in
a way in which the minimal amount of pain is inflicted on
the fewest people, and that, hopefully, some kind of mutual
understanding and perhaps growth will result from the
endeavor. I acknowledge anger and frustration, my own as
well as yours, *but it will not have the upper hand.* In all
honesty, I do not know how much it is possible to achieve
in this day and age and culture, but we'll see. We'll see how
far we can go within the framework of our own limited
humanity. Is that acceptable to you? . . . Judith."

I nod assent, too choked with emotion to respond verbally. We get out into the frozen air, extract John's suitcase
from the trunk, and walk stiffly to the bar in the terminal
building. The television monitor informs us, with an an-

noying oscillation, that the plane will depart on schedule and boards at Gate 6 in fifteen minutes. John orders us each a brandy. The rest is a distracted daze of milling people and poorly disguised de-personalization.

John checks his ticket and baggage. The hostess points to the security check-post, and we stop at a sign that says NO VISITORS BEYOND THIS POINT. We embrace and John starts up the incline.

"John."

He hesitates and looks back.

"John."

Someone says, "Madam, you're not allowed to—" and then there are only John's lips and touch and smell and warmth and wholeness around me, giving, taking.

"John, I'm sorry. I love you. I love you. I—"

"Sh-h-h. My love, my darling. I know, I know."

The envelope is addressed in a large, printed, childlike hand to DR. JUDY BENETAR with a small pressed flower glued over the seal.

January 10th
3.00 A.M.

Dear Judy-Dr. Benetar,

I am leaving this letter on my pillow for the nurses to find so that you wont worry about me. I wanted to talk to you at our next cession (how do you spell that?) but I have to leave all of a sudden. I'll give you some of my reasons in a minite, but first I want to thank you for working so hard with me.

Wait. I'm going to find my dictionery. Okay, I have it.

I will miss you, but maybe if I get things straitened out in a hurry, I will see you soon. Well, I guess you want to know why I left. Here are my reasons. There are some good ones and some bad ones. I hope you dont get mad about the bad ones.

1. Remember I told you I went to the woods last year and asked the wind to send me a leaf for you and I couldnt catch one? Well, I thought one of the reasons the wind didnt send me a leaf for you was because it really wanted me to ask for a leaf for myself. So I want to go and find out.

2. I'm tired of being cooped up on the ward. Everyone is very nice, but its so shut in, like the inside of an egg shell.

3. Treek said he was going to poison everybody and it would be my fault if I stayed.

4. Sue-Ann got sick and vomited last nite and they had to call the surgens (surgeons, the dictionery says. That doesnt make any sense at all). So I know Treek isnt kidding. The nurses told us she might have to go down to a surgical ward for awhile. I looked at her and she looked awful. When I went in her room, she wouldnt talk to me so she must know I did it. I already killed one person. Joanna. I'm not going to stay around and let Treek kill any more. I can feel the poison building up again.

5. I know I made a contract with you that I wouldnt cut myself anymore. You said there were better ways to get rid of the poison, like talking. Well, it didnt work. Sue-Ann is sick. I wont cut myself because I promised you, but I have to go away from people until it goes away. Especially you. If I kill you with my poison that would be the worst crime I ever committed because all your other patients would suffer. And you are the one in the most danger because you get the most exposure to my poison and you come the closest. And I love you more than anyone.

6. Somebody better could use this bed.

Treek says if we dont go soon it will be too late. Its

starting to get light outside. I hope you all dont get too
mad at me. Please explain to the nurses.

Love,

ELAINE

I look around at the solemn faces in the nurses' station.
I read them the letter.

"Angela, stop crying," I say.

"It's my fault, Judy!" she wails. "God, I should have
known after that announcement about Sue-Ann. I should
have known!"

"What could you have done?" I ask quietly.

"I could have locked the ward, if I'd guessed she might
leave, for one thing."

"Angela, you can't berate yourself for not getting into
somebody else's head. Elaine could have reacted in any one
of a number of ways to Sue-Ann's illness. And as for lock-
ing the ward, you have to remember that Elaine's a veteran
of about ten to fifteen hospitals. She'd have found a way to
get out if she were really determined."

"Well, I could have spent more time with her last night,"
Angela protests, wiping her nose.

I nod.

"Sure you could," I say, "and I'm sure you could have
spent more time with fifteen other patients who *didn't*
elope from the ward. You can only do what you can do.
You're not a magician. These things happen."

"She didn't give me any indication she was any more
upset than anyone else or I would have called you. There
were just no clues. She must have written that note under
a blanket with a flashlight or something, cause I made a
floor check about four and didn't notice anything odd."

Angela sits down, looking tired and empty, and I spend
another half-hour consoling her and myself. My mind re-
works recent sessions with Elaine, looking for therapeutic
errors in perception or judgment, and I make a silent list

of questions to go over with one or maybe both of my
supervisors plus Mel Bernstein for the value of different
perspectives.

The rest of the morning is spent in making various un-
productive phone attempts to trace Elaine, seeing other
patients, and trying to find another resident to switch a
night on call with me.

Sally, the occupational therapist, catches me between
patients.

"Judy, will you have a word with Beth, please? She's
refusing to come to o.t."

"Just tell her it's required," I answer, pausing in writing
up some notes.

"I did, but she won't."

"Shit. Sure, Sally, okay, I'll give it a try."

Beth is sitting at the desk in her four-bedded room, pretending to look at a magazine. She turns a page when I walk
in, and I prepare myself for an emotional struggle.

Since the night Beth started eating, the power struggle
that had centered around whether she would live or die had
been translated into various verbal and nonverbal com-
munications. Sessions with her had alternated between a
tacit cooperative alliance with me to seek out major stum-
bling blocks in her ability to function, or a kind of teasing,
angry, resistant mutism.

The staff had encouraged her to participate fully in all
ward activities almost from the moment she had assumed
responsibility for feeding herself. These periods, which
involved interactions with several other people, had allowed Beth an opportunity to experiment with some of the
different feelings and problems she had had with the major
figures in her life, i.e., her mother, father, and her maternal
grandfather. She had been obstinate and difficult at times,
charming and helpful at others. Today looks as if it's going
to be a difficult one for her and us.

"Beth, what the hell is this all about?"

She looks up from a photograph of a model kneeling beside a poodle. "What's all what about?" she asks innocently.

"Sally says you won't go to o.t. If you remember, the staff struck a bargain with you some weeks ago. You participate voluntarily in all ward activities and we would agree to treat you here in this facility. So what's going on? What's this about o.t.?" I repeat, in a hurry to get this over with so I can return to my other work. I wait for the argument.

"It's about nothing. Okay, I'll go," she says flippantly, closing the magazine. She gets up with a toss of her now silky black hair and without another word walks out of the room with a smirk on her face.

I stand there bewildered and pissed for a minute. Then on the way back to the nurses' station it dawns on me that that was exactly the point of the whole operation—that I be bewildered and pissed. I go back to my notes, shaking my head and laughing under my breath. An aide asks to be let in on the joke.

"She's too much!" I say, bursting, and I fill him in on Beth's antics.

He shares an anecdote from his own experience with Beth that happened the previous night when they had had dinner at the same table in the day room.

Beth had said, "Ralph, I think one of the nurses was looking for you."

He had gotten up to inquire and went looking for the three different nurses on duty. When he returned, Beth had smiled and made small talk. She asked him if he went to college besides working as an aide and told him some stories from her college days. He had found her unusually friendly and conversational, but had a feeling of something being a little off. Then Ralph had noticed Beth's plate, which had been full when he'd left, but now was empty, with what was left of the gravy dripping suspiciously off one edge. He made a casual comment about how quickly she'd eaten, to which she'd responded with a hasty nod.

Then she had said, "Well, excuse me. I have a few things to wash out," and had stacked her dishes on the trolley and left the room.

Ralph had found the whole meal under some clean, crumpled-up paper towels in the trash can. He'd reported it to the nurses, who were going to pass on the information at rounds that afternoon.

As Ralph is talking, I find myself contrasting the wasted, filthy, unresponsive, twenty-seven-year-old urchin brought in by the police only two months ago with her lice and her open sores with this openly mischievous, hostile woman trying to work something through for herself in the rather deadly serious games she's been playing with us. Though the process has been in some ways obscure, it has also seemed to follow a peculiar kind of logic, about which we have begun to get a sense as we have lived and worked and related with her. Ralph finishes his narrative by referring to the mixed feelings of frustration and amusement she has aroused in him.

"Yes, I know what you're talking about," I say with a laugh. "Thanks, Ralph. That's a help to know. She's obviously into something we'll have to deal a lot more with in sessions."

"By the way," he adds, "her mother's been doing a lot of sabotaging of our work lately. Have you heard about that?"

"Yes, unless there's something new. You mean that after weeks of calling Beth a 'spiteful bitch,' she's now started a 'What are they doing to you, my poor baby' routine?"

"Yes, that's what I meant," he says disgustedly. "The other night, Mrs. Sloan came here dressed like a hooker in mourning with a guy she said was her cousin, and in front of Beth, she says to him, 'Look at her! Can you believe that's the girl you saw last year? Just look at her, Will, how pale she is and all!' And then she does this crying routine on his shoulder."

I tell Ralph of my fruitless attempts to get Beth to agree to family sessions.

"In lieu of family therapy," I continue, "I've thought of severely restricting the mother's visits and inviting her to have her own individual sessions with Lois Birnbaum, while I continue to work with Beth." Lois is the social worker.

Sally sticks her head around the corner, waiting to be noticed.

"What is it now, Sally?"

She makes a face.

"Not Beth again?"

"Who else?"

"Oh, c'mon, Sally, what is this?" I grimace.

"Judy, cross my heart, I'm not sticking pins in her. I haven't even strangled her yet. But guess what she's *doing* in o.t. today?" Sally bats her thick lashes.

"I give up."

"She's taken a piece of brown wrapping paper and one black crayon and sat down at one of the big tables, closed her eyes, and started scribbling. When I confronted her about it, she said it was modern art."

"Maybe it is," I say hopefully.

"Bullshit!" Sally protests. "Have you ever seen the beautiful needlepoint and embroidery she's done? She knows what she's doing and it ain't modern art, believe me. She's out to get us, honey!"

"Yeah, I know," I sigh. "It's part of the whole thing she's up against and I guess she's going to have to deal with it her own way. Well, don't fall for it, Sally. She'd love it if you'd fly into a rage."

"So I should just ignore it for now?" she asks.

"More or less. You can sort of let her know you're on to her, then make a few sincere suggestions for alternatives that might be more interesting and creative, but I'd leave it at that for now and not fall into the trap."

Sally tosses her Shirley Temple curls and says uncertainly, "Okay-y," drawing out the word, "but I hope you start taking this up with her soon. She's driving me crazy!"

She returns to the o.t. room, doing a ridiculous rhumba, knowing that Ralph and I are watching her. With a kick and a circular wave, she disappears out of sight. I finally manage to finish my notes and leave for lunch with an old friend.

Rosa has arrived at the English-style pub ahead of me. She stands outside in the cold, huddled into an antique raccoon coat. Her head is buried in a muffler, and she doesn't see me get out of the taxi. Her marvelous auburn hair has been partially subdued by a brown, home-knit hat that she has pulled protectively down over her ears.

"Rosa, you nut! Why didn't you wait inside?"

"I like this weather. It's so crisp!" she says from somewhere inside the muffler. The dark eyes that look over the top are unusually without makeup.

We turn into the dark warmth of the pub and Janis Joplin on the jukebox. Rosa unwinds her muffler, stuffs it in a sleeve of her coat, and pulls off the hat, which she folds into a hidden pocket. The rich, long hair tumbles over her shoulders as she hangs the coat on the wooden rack over mine.

We sit at a round table across from each other. The waiter comes and we order two dark beers. We stare at each other and at the table and share a silence that says where do we begin after a couple of years?

Rosa and Paul had spent some difficult evenings with us just before Ben and I split. I hadn't been in touch with them since then. They'd been thinking of buying a house on the island owned by one of Paul's law partners. They'd been having trouble too, but had been less open about the problems, and led us to believe there was nothing serious to worry about.

It is rather striking to see Rosa dressed so simply in slacks and a turtleneck, and a certain tension that had tightened her face in the past is noticeably absent.

"You look well, Rosa."

She swallows some beer and smiles.

"I am," she says, then puts down her glass, folds her arms on the table, and adds gently, "I heard about you and Ben. I don't know whether to say I'm sorry or congratulate you. Depends on where you're at with it. You're looking well, too, so I assume things are going okay."

I nod and fill her in on some of the missing time. She listens attentively, interrupting once in a while to ask a question. Her presence has a noticeably different quality, more settled and aware than I'd remembered her.

"Did you know that Paul and I split too?" Rosa asks.

"No, when?"

"Oh, I guess not long after you." She stops to consider, "But, god, it seems longer than that! I'm in such a different place now!"

We order two more beers and decide to split a sausage and pepper sandwich.

"So what are you into?" I ask, watching her face.

Rosa stares thoughtfully into her glass and answers, "A lot. So much has happened, I hardly know where to begin. Let's see . . ."

She starts counting things off on her fingers as she talks: "I finally finished my dissertation, and I'm teaching a course at the New School; Daphne just had four puppies; Paul got remarried in August, and his wife is expecting; my sister's studying in Geneva and sounds happy in her letters; my parents retired to Arizona—they hate it, they're dying of boredom, and they'll probably be back in the city before I even get used to not having them around; and Anne and I moved to a new apartment on West End Avenue two weeks ago. It's a super place with a great view of the river."

"Who's Anne?"

"The woman I've been living with for the last six months. The woman I love."

"Oh," I say with open surprise. Two years ago, she had been deciding with Paul whether to have two or three kids and if it was premature to think about buying a station wagon. But the mystery of her change in attitude begins to fall into place. Rosa has obviously found a life style with which she is comparatively content.

"How's it going? Sounds like a pretty far cry from Paul," I say.

The waiter comes with the sandwich and drinks. We put the plate in the middle, and I slice the thick, Italian bread in half.

Rosa takes a bite, licks her fingers, and says, "It's fantastic. I've never known anything like it. Do you really want to hear, Judy? I mean, we've been out of touch for a long time and a lot of important things have happened—I don't know where you're at with some of these issues."

I put down my half of the sandwich and answer, "I really want to hear."

Rosa comes to life and says with elation, "It's just really incredible. All the things I always looked for with a man I've found with Anne. We have such good times. We read together, we walk for miles in the country on weekends with the dogs, we attend a lot of women's conferences, we share the housework and cooking, we love and laugh and cry and get angry without ever losing touch with each other. And the sex is something else. It's really tender and caring and mutual, and there's such an intuitive knowing how to satisfy. I've given up so much of my old shit; it just isn't relevant or necessary anymore. You know, like faking orgasms half the time and being afraid to say what gives me pleasure. It's just so free and loving, Judy. I don't think I've ever been this happy."

"You look it," I reiterate. "You're radiant."

She adds, "But it's been tough a lot of the time. We've

gotten a lot of flak in social situations. In the beginning, we were so caught up in our own defensiveness, we probably alienated some people unnecessarily. But it's gotten better. As we've become more tolerant, so have others, for the most part."

Rosa sips her beer for some minutes, lost in her own thoughts, then looks up suddenly and says, "Where are you in terms of the women's movement?"

I consider. "Aware, empathetic, but not politically active. Unless you consider discussing women's issues as they arise in a therapy session politically active."

Rosa asks quietly, "Could you give me an example?"

"Probably many, if I really gave it some thought." I tell her about a session with Nancy and describe some of the women's issues that repeatedly appear in different sessions.

In conclusion, I summarize, "Essentially, then, what recurrently intrudes on her ability to function well and creatively is her readiness to sabotage her talent and integrity by forming essentially shallow, overly dependent relationships with men who put her down for wanting something for herself. Now granted, that's partly her own personal historical pathology, but certainly part of that pathology is culturally determined, and I've discussed it with her from both points of view."

Rosa has been listening carefully. When I pick up my drink, she says, "Yes, I'd consider that politically active, even if you hadn't thought about it that way. You mentioned 'pathology,' and that made me think of something else I wanted to ask you. Do you consider a relationship like Anne's and mine necessarily pathological?"

"No," I answer, taking a bite of my sandwich.

"A lot of shrinks do. Well," she persists, "what *is* your point of view about it? I'm asking for a reason, Judy, I'm not just cross-examining. I know you're still in training, but I was thinking of referring somebody to you for treatment, through the hospital, if it can be worked out satisfactorily that way. She really could use some help, but she's been through a lousy analysis and is simply terrified of being fucked-over again. Also, I'd really like to know what your thoughts are on the issue."

Rosa and I turn back to our glasses. She starts nibbling at the crumbs on the plate, waiting for my response.

"Well, without getting too heady about it," I say, "I guess I think that all kinds of relationships are possible and work-able. I think there are reasons why certain relationships are formed, but I'd be reluctant to label them 'pathological' unless the people involved in the relationship were being seriously destructive to themselves or each other. . . . Rosa, the plate isn't edible! I'm still hungry, too. Why don't we order another sandwich?"

"Great!" she says, and looks around for the waiter, who clears our empty dishes and takes the order for more drinks and food.

"So, then," Rosa muses, "you don't see as one of your goals in treatment, returning people to the values of tradi-tional middle-class life?"

"It would only be one of my goals if that's what they were looking for. Some people want that, you know."

I pause, waiting for a protest, but Rosa says simply, "I suppose. It's hard for me to believe that anyone would really *want* that, if they were fully aware of the alterna-tives, but basically I dig what you're trying to say. And if somebody gay came to you for treatment, you wouldn't take it as a foregone conclusion that you'd have to make an attempt to analyze them back to a heterosexual existence?"

"No. As with anyone who might come to me with a problem," I speculate, "I'd listen to what they thought was the problem, explore it with them, and hopefully reflect back to them what their feelings were about it. I think it's a foregone conclusion that serious problems can arise for a person in any relationship, be it homo-, hetero-, or bisex-ual. And the essential issue for me is to help define what the areas of difficulty are, so that the person can get some relief from them—rather than to get someone to eventually conform to any preconceived notions that I might have about the way relationships should be to be called healthy."

"Do you have any?" Rosa asks.

"What? Preconceived notions?"

She nods.

"I try to avoid them. They're all suspect!"

We laugh as the waiter returns with our order. He hesitates before he leaves, looks at Rosa and says, "I hope you don't mind my saying this, but you have the most beautiful hair I've ever seen."

Rosa's face is a play of conflicting emotions. She looks back at him for evidence of a come-on, which seems to be nonexistent. His expression is open and sensitive. He turns to leave, and Rosa makes some kind of inner decision.

"Thanks," she says with a hint of merriment. "Yours is nice, too."

Understanding the nuance, he smiles without malice and resumes his work.

Rosa looks over at me and says, "A few months ago, I probably wouldn't have asked myself any questions about who he was or where he was coming from. I just woulda slugged him."

After lunch, an initial interview with a new patient recalls the discussion with Rosa, and I find myself wondering about the different degrees to which women's issues enter into therapeutic sessions. For this woman, they will obviously be vital, as well as the issues involved in her own personal history.

Martha Wickham is a twenty-five-year-old woman who has been married to an associate professor of English at City College for two years and has a six-month-old baby. She has never been in therapy before, and when I ask her why she has sought help at this point in her life, she bursts into tears.

Opening a drawer of the desk, I find a box of tissues and hand them to her. Through her sobs, she nods an acknowledgment and blows her nose. Her straight, light-brown hair is secured in a stringy pony tail with a thick rubber band, and her wedding ring looks too small for her pudgy fingers. She sighs heavily, wipes away her tears, and looks past me out the window with tired brown eyes.

Then, angrily, she turns to me and says, "Why did I come for therapy? Look at me, for Christ's sake!" indicating with a sweep of her hands the utilitarian, shapeless gray jumper, coarse support stockings, and muddied rubber boots.

Having made a beginning, her words start to tumble out all over one another in an effort to get it all said as quickly as possible.

"I've never looked like this before in my life! I've gained forty pounds in about a year and a half. I can't stand myself! And I can't stop eating, either. Jeff, my husband, doesn't say very much, but he must hate it, too. Or maybe he just doesn't care. I don't know, I don't know what to think anymore. We hardly talk to each other. Would you believe I was once voted the prettiest girl in my class at college? Look at me now! It's disgusting! Except for the baby, it's torture to get up every day. If it weren't for her, I think I'd —well, I don't know what I'd do."

She lapses into a troubled silence and I repeat quietly, "But why now? I understand what you're saying, but some of these problems have apparently been around for a while. What I'm trying to get at is why you decided to come here today, as opposed, say, to a month ago or a year ago."

She thinks for a minute and then answers soberly, "I guess because of the thing with my mother-in-law. That was kind of like the straw that broke the camel's back."

Martha then goes on to explain her husband's recent repeated requests to have his mother live with them. His father had died about a year ago, and since then, the sixty-four-year-old woman had been living with Jeff's sister, who now plans to move to California. Martha describes her mother-in-law as a whining, selfish hypochondriac, who will neither accept an offer to live with an aging aunt nor take a place of her own, though she has the financial means to do so.

"When I try to explain my reservations to Jeff, he just calls me heartless and cold," she moans. "But *I'll* be the one who'll have to take care of her. And that will make five people I'll be taking care of. I don't really think I can handle any more."

"Who are the other four?" I ask.

Martha then goes on to detail a history of growing up with an alcoholic mother and a crippled father, who had lost the use of his legs following an industrial accident when she was nine. Since then, Martha, the eldest of three children, had taken over much of the responsibility for her brother and sister, and later, as her mother's drinking got worse and her father's depression more severe, she had assumed the burden of caring for them also. After her siblings had graduated from high school, Martha had begun to enjoy life for the first time. She did well in college and began to "make up for lost time socially and sexually."

One summer, she had saved enough money to take a trip to Europe. The vacation had been idyllic, and on the boat back to the States she'd met Jeff. They had married two months later. Martha's description of her husband sounds one-dimensional and incomplete, almost an unconscious caricature of the tweedy, pipe-smoking, handsomely profiled English professor.

Half a year into their marriage, Jeff had asked his wife to quit her job as a copy editor, complaining that she was always too tired after work to cook a decent meal or take a "real interest" in him and his work. Reluctantly, Martha had agreed. Her parents had taken advantage of the situation, and had begun calling her over anything that could be interpreted as a crisis in their lives. With her new "free time," it also became clear to her that the role her husband had in mind for her was not exactly the one she'd planned for herself.

"I asked him once, straight out, what he wanted from a wife. Without even stopping to think, he said, 'I want someone to meet me at the door, smiling, with a cocktail freshly made; someone who asks me about my work and interests; who'll give me children and help entertain my friends.' "

"Has Jeff ever asked what you wanted?"

Martha stops to think a minute, biting her lower lip. "No, I don't think he has," she answers, slightly surprised at the realization.

So, as they had settled into their married routine, Martha learned through various verbal and nonverbal messages that things were smoother if she did not articulate her own needs or wants, and in fact, it is obvious from the interview that she has almost forgotten that she has desires of her own. Since the baby was born, Martha has literally had no time to herself. During her pregnancy, she had eaten voraciously and continued to do so after the birth of her daughter, never regaining her ante-partum weight.

As the hour begins to wane, I summarize, "So, if your mother-in-law moves in with you, you'll be taking care of her, your husband, your parents, and the baby. . . . Who takes care of you?"

She shrugs her shoulders, then adds in a flat voice that Jeff has recently put a down payment on a house in Long Island and she feels like she's moving into a coffin for the rest of her life.

Her expression changes, and her eyes search mine. "Does any of what I've said make any sense to you?"

I laugh and answer lightly, "Almost too much!"

Martha looks puzzled.

I explain. "People don't become doctors for nothing.

Among other things, I know firsthand what it feels like to 'take care of' almost everyone else in my life!"

As she smiles in appreciation, I add, "But guess what?"

She looks up.

"During the last couple of years, I've discovered that I count, too."

We both laugh, and I ask her if she has any questions to ask me.

Martha says hesitantly, "I don't know whether it's fair to ask, but could you tell me a little bit about therapy? I don't know much about it."

"What do you want to know?"

"I don't know—it's really hard to say. In cartoons, you always see this picture of a bearded man with glasses sitting behind some patient lying on a couch. That's sort of bothered me. I'd like to be able to see who I'm talking to. . . ."

I scan briefly for her the different therapeutic modalities, ranging from the classical Freudian analytic situation she has described to the newer, more sensational approaches, then reiterate that I am still in training and though I may draw upon several of the theories to which I've been exposed, I have no dogmatic bias at this point.

"Would therapy with you be anything like this last hour?" Martha asks.

"Yes, except that I may have more to say from time to time. Today you had a lot to get off your chest. Why do you ask?"

Martha laughs nervously. "I don't know—it's hard to explain. But it was kind of a surprise to find you so—'human,' is that the word? It's hard to believe you're really a doctor somehow."

"Some people find that hard to deal with. If you do, I'd like to remind you again that you don't have to settle for the first therapist you're sent to. You can shop around and see some of the other people in the department, if you like. How *you* feel in a therapeutic setting is really important.

Would you like to think it over a while?"

She makes a decision and shakes her head. "No. I'd like to make another appointment with you for next week. One of the best things was that I felt I could say anything to you. I need that. It's such a relief. I don't know what the connection is, but I just thought to myself, 'Maybe I can really start on a diet now and stick to it.' "

I get out my appointment book and mention casually, "It's not too hard to figure out the connection. There are all kinds of 'food' in this world."

Martha puzzles over the remark while we try to agree upon a regular appointment time. She pulls on a dull brown coat with dark leather buttons. With her hand on the doorknob, she stops and says, "Oh!"

Turning, she says with a wide smile, "Thanks for the meal!"

Toward the end of January, I am able to write John that my literary agent has negotiated a contract with a publisher, and I've met with the editor. In the letter, it is some consolation to describe my anxieties about being in print:

How, darling, do I even begin to describe in black and white things that barely lend themselves to description? Things like feelings, nuance, inflection, immediacy? The richness and subtlety of exchange between two people in a single moment could fill volumes. And I am going to be so presumptuous as to attempt to describe part of a life style that involves several people on many different levels? Frankly, the prospect makes me only too aware of my own limitations. I am frightened, humbled, and paralyzed for the time being. I am quite clear that at best, I will only come somewhere close to what I'm trying to do. I know what you were talking about now. When it was just a piece of writing I was doing for myself, to stave off the loneliness, perhaps, it had a different flavor. I knew intimately what I was writing about; i.e., I was talking to myself, sorting some things out, as it were. But to assume the responsibility of saying something meaningful to other people, some of whom have had no contact with the world in which I function; to sign a contract and have the whole thing become a businesslike situation is rather different, I think, from what I'd anticipated.

I want to show that psychiatrists are people, too. I want to take me and other shrinks out of the category of priests, gurus, witch doctors, etcetera, who are supposed to be above and beyond ordinary human vulnerability and interactions, which is bullshit, pure and simple. Sure, my training and experience make me able to help people through some of their hangups and get a sense of their own autonomy.

Despite my ability and training, I have my own hangups, my own sets of difficulties with autonomy, needs, hungers. In short, I'm human, and I think people should know that, even if it's hard to hear. It's a mistake to set shrinks apart from other people by virtue of their profession. In fact, it's often my awareness of my own struggles, my own past experience, that enables me to identify with and help other people through an impasse.

I can't be any more definitive than I feel. And I'm still working a lot of things through for myself. A good deal of what I do with patients is not, in fact, new. It draws from other, often far more learned people in the field, *plus* my own sense of what I'm about. But at any rate, *who* I am as a person is central to my work. And like most other people, much of me is questioning, grappling. I'd like to think I can share some of my personal struggles with the reader without losing authenticity. Unless people are completely closed, and I don't want to believe that, it doesn't take much looking around to know that our culture's in serious trouble. So why shouldn't I include some of my own questioning, or fumbling if you will, in the manuscript? Well, we'll see.

Miss you. It's hard to believe it's only been a little over a month since I saw you. Write soon, Love.

I unlock the office door for Beth's session. Her progress over the past weeks has been stormy and erratic, including one major regression to fully withdrawn catatonia and another few days of tube feedings. Because of the ward administrator's unusual tolerance and understanding, I have been able to obtain a second extension period for her, of which she has three weeks left.

She comes into the office, selects a chair that puts her neither opposite nor next to me, and stares at her manicured toenails. I wait. Today she is dressed in white clam-diggers, a black V-neck sweater, and Japanese rubber thong sandals.

Fifteen or twenty minutes go by, and tired of my own boredom, I finally say, "This fascinating dialogue's just blowing my mind. Could you talk a little slower, please? I can't keep up with you."

Beth fights her mirth, but eventually laughs out loud. Then she collects herself and returns to her toenail inspection.

"Well, if you don't feel like talking today," I say more seriously, "we can stop now. There are some other things I could be doing with this time."

I start to get to my feet, when she looks up and signals me to stop.

"Wait a minute," she orders. "I'll get it together. Just give me a few seconds." She runs a hand through her hair and says sarcastically, "So what should we talk about? The life cycle of the amoeba?"

"Is that what you feel like? An amoeba?" I ask.

She laughs nervously. "Yeah, I guess so."

I define: "A formless blob that reacts to external stimuli and keeps changing its shape in response to the environment? Seems to me there's more to you than that."

"Well, you're wrong," she says defiantly.

"Okay, if you say so," I concur casually.

Beth sits up in surprise. "Hey," she protests, "you're not supposed to agree with that! You know I'm not an amoeba!"

"Oh. I see. Well, what am I *supposed* to do, Beth? Argue with you about it so we can get into another power struggle again? Frankly, I'm getting a little tired of being set up. It never gets us very far. And personally, you don't need to convince me that I can't *make* you accept anything you don't want to accept. I believe it."

She bites thoughtfully into her knuckles and decides on another direction. "When are you and the staff gonna decide to discharge me? I'm getting sick and tired of this funny farm and I want to get out of here."

"Nobody's forcing you to stay," I remind her.

"I know," she whines, "but I don't want to sign out against medical advice. Why don't you and the nurses think I'm ready to leave?"

"We've been through all that before, Beth. What is there about it that you don't understand?"

She angrily lapses into her tirade about psychiatrists and how they always think they know what's best for you. The crucial issues that have held up her discharge have had largely to do with her steadfast refusal to accept any post-hospital follow-up program. Neither would she consider the alternative of plans for work or return to school. She has maintained a fixed adherence to the idea of returning to the same room in the same hotel as her mother and has insisted that all she needs is a rest from her "hospital ordeal" and then will be all right again. The issue has been complicated by the fact that this, too, has become a power struggle, and Beth clearly feels she has an investment in "winning" apart from what might be rational or of some real value to her.

I make an attempt to point this out to her and also to discuss some of the implications of moving back in with her mother, and I allude briefly to the danger of regressing to another catatonic state because she has not yet been able to examine or deal with some of the issues that precipitated her hospitalization or regressions.

She dismisses the conversations as "bullshit" and says petulantly, "Well, you're going to have to discharge me soon, anyway. My extension time is up in three weeks."

"Yes, that's true," I admit. "And let's hope you won't have won the rather questionable victory of having cut off your nose to spite your face."

I hold the door open for her and confirm the time of our next appointment. She nods nonchalantly and walks down to the day room.

Getting off the elevator, I run into Dr. White, who asks me about Beth. I bring him roughly up to date.

"It's almost a shame she decided to talk and eat on her own," he comments, shaking his head solemnly.

"What on earth makes you say that, Dr. White?" I ask in surprise.

He purses his lips and proclaims with a rather pompous, annoying certainty, "She'll regress. You'll see. She has already in the hospital, and she will again. I've had a few catatonics in the course of my career. There's only one way to treat 'em as far as I'm concerned. A course of twenty to forty shock treatments usually does the trick, followed in some cases with maintenance shock every month or so."

He notices my expressions and says, "Don't take my word for it! Read the experts. Read Kalinowsky, my girl! It's the only way to get a lasting remission. The mistake most people make is not to give enough; it has to be from twenty to forty. And they'll thank you in the end. They know what really helps 'em. You're really doing that woman a disservice in a way. But you're still in training, I guess you can be forgiven. . . ."

He chuckles heartily and slaps me on the back.

"Well, keep up the good work," he says, "I guess you're one of the ones who has to learn the hard way! So long, doc!"

He pushes past me onto the elevator, smiling expansively.

The end of winter has dragged itself miserably into March and refused to give any indication of letting go. Despite Dr. White's dire predictions, Beth and I seem to have worked out a temporarily workable compromise.

After her discharge from the hospital, she moved back into her mother's hotel. But despite her refusal to find other accommodation or to participate in a day program, so far she has kept every outpatient appointment, three times a week, working on her problems with varying degrees of motivation, but as yet, with no major setbacks.

I turn from a memory of her laughing an hour ago to Stan's current resistance to talk about anything meaningful to him, making a pretense of attending carefully to his monotonous obsessions about college courses and career choices and vaguely wondering what I can do to bring him back to a feeling level.

It is hard to imagine the treetops outside the window turning green in a few weeks. The wind blows, and they scrape against the pane. There is a gentle knock on the door. Gwen, the secretary-receptionist, apologizes for interrupting and calls me out of the room. Intrusions on a session are rare and seldom without good cause. Concerned, I excuse myself to Stan and join Gwen in the corridor, closing the door behind me.

"I'm really sorry to disturb you, Judy, but it sounds like

it might be an emergency. There's some woman crying on the phone. I couldn't make out most of what she was saying, but she kept begging me to put you on the phone. I tried to tell her to call back between sessions, but she said she was calling long-distance and it was a matter of life and death."

We had been walking toward Gwen's desk. She hands me one of her two phones and pushes the appropriate button. I pick up the receiver and identify myself.

"Dr. Benetar? Judy?" a voice questions between sobs. Then there is a sound as though the phone has been dropped on the other end, a scramble to retrieve it, and a lot of screaming and crying. It occurs to me with a jolt who it is.

"Elaine? Elaine, is that you?"

I hear a garbled assent and then more hysterics. I try to make my voice sound firm and forceful and not communicate my growing anxiety.

"Elaine, now calm down and try to make some sense. I can't understand a thing you're saying. Elaine, stop it now. C'mon."

The volume gradually subsides and I am able to ask where she is.

"In Delaware."

I dimly recall that she has a married sister in Delaware.

"Judy, I have to see you. Can I see you?"

When she collects herself enough to be coherent, she tells me she'll be back in New York by the middle of the week. I give her an appointment for Wednesday afternoon. She sounds exhausted and subdued by the time she hangs up.

I replace the receiver and say to the outpatients' secretary, "Thanks for calling me out, Gwen. It *was* important. That was Elaine Carson. You know her, don't you?"

"Yes, sure. I won't ask you how she is. Anyway, you're welcome. It's almost an art to separate out the really serious calls from the ones that can wait. Maybe I should ask for a raise?"

Gwen returns to her typing.

I walk slowly back to the office, preoccupied with questions and worries about Elaine. Apart from a hurried note that said "I'M OKAY," it has been nearly three months since I last heard from her.

As I close the door and sit down, Stan puts a small pouch of tobacco into his shoulder bag and lights a cigarette.

"I'm sorry, Stan. You were talking about forestry, I think."

After a long pause, he says disconnectedly, "Yeah, right. . . . Well, I . . ."

I look up, mildly startled by his silence. "Is anything wrong?" I ask.

"Um, no, I don't think so. I just feel funny about going on. Maybe we should stop and I'll talk about forestry next time."

He flicks an ash into the wastebasket, looking withdrawn and guarded.

"What is it you feel funny about?"

He grows clearly anxious and starts shifting around uncomfortably in the chair. His obvious distress brings me back to the task at hand.

"I don't know—never mind," he says nervously, his eyes looking for help.

I offer, "Want to do yourself a favor?"

He nods quickly.

"Get into it, the feeling funny."

Small beads of sweat have appeared on Stan's brow. He pulls a tissue from the box and wipes them away. His hand trembles slightly.

"Okay," he says, "here goes nothing."

He puts down his cigarette and begins. "I feel funny about going on because you seem so out of it. I think you're still into that phone call or whatever it was."

"And . . . ?" I encourage.

"And, well, I feel like you've got a lot of important things on your mind. I mean, you *have* to. You're a doctor, and you've got a lot of things to do and think about. So I figure maybe forestry can wait until next week." He begins to gather his belongings.

"Stan," I say, "apart from what you 'figure,' how does it make you *feel*, my seeming preoccupied with a phone call in the middle of your session?"

"Feel? I don't know, sort of left out, I guess," he tries, sitting back in the chair and forgetting about leaving momentarily.

"Abandoned?" I ask.

"Yeah, I suppose. Left out, abandoned, kind of cheated in a way. Betrayed, maybe," he adds anxiously.

"Okay. And how does all that make you feel?" I continue.

"I don't know what you're getting at," he says.

"Well, maybe it would be easier if you thought about it a little abstractly. Just imagine someone, anyone, who kind of 'bares his soul' to another person. And the other person abandons, cheats, and betrays him. What effect do you think it would have?"

He looks puzzled, then his face takes on a curious, almost horrified expression.

"You mean anger?" he asks, incredulous.

"Why not? It seems to me I'd be furious if I felt that somebody had treated me that way."

"But I couldn't get angry with you," he says, a look of disbelief still on his face.

"Why not?"

Stan gets up and walks around the room. Then he leans against the wall, with his hands in the back pockets of his jeans, staring at the floor, thinking.

"Because . . ." he says and stops. Then he looks up and blurts out, "Because you'd turn off, go away like—oh shit, like my old lady!"

He resumes his seat, regains some of his composure and says, "Well, it sounds good, but I don't really feel any anger toward you in *here*," pointing to his chest. "I don't feel much of anything as a matter of fact."

"Okay. Right, well, you're the only one who knows what you feel," I respond. "So, see you next week, then, same time."

He asks me for a number where he can leave a message in case he has to cancel the following week's appointment. I tear a piece of paper from a yellow pad and write down the number of the general office of the department of psychiatry.

As I hand it to him, he says, "You know, that's really unprofessional, man."

"What, Stan?"

"Scrawling your number on some dinky piece of paper. You ought to have special stationery or a card for things like this. Like, that's really unprofessional."

I have to smile as I see him to the door.

"You don't get angry," I reiterate. "You just imply that your shrink is unprofessional and threaten to cancel your next appointment."

The remark stops him in his tracks. "My God," he says, startled, "I pull this kind of shit all the time! That's wild! I don't get 'angry' at people, I just stab them in the back! Holy shit!" After a moment of assimilation, he throws his head back and laughs.

Without warning, he takes my hand in both of his and says with a wide grin, "We swing sometimes, baby! See ya!" and trots off down the hall.

My enjoyment of his relief is tempered by the nagging echo of Elaine's call.

Nancy fidgets through three-quarters of her session. She again plays at being a "good patient," running through lists of things she's begun to do for herself and making remarks that sound insightful and perceptive but that have a curious rehearsed, flat, atonal quality. Finally she snaps shut the clasp on her handbag, with which her fingers have been playing since the beginning of the hour.

"Well," she says decisively, "there's nothing to do but to do it! I want to stop therapy. I've been seeing you for over a year, and I think I know pretty well what my major problems are. What I have to do now is go out and see if I can stand on my own two feet. I don't want to have to rely on you to help me solve every little difficulty, and—hell, what I'm trying to say is that I don't want to come anymore, for a while, anyway. Maybe I'll see how it goes for a month or two and then I'll give you a call. Okay?"

She looks up tentatively, relieved to have gotten it out, but partly anticipating some fantasied retaliation.

"Okay," I agree. "It often happens that people want to 'take vacations' from their psychiatrists for various reasons, some of which get stated, some not. I just wonder if you'd care to spend some time exploring why now, at this particular point in your therapy?"

"Yeek!" Nancy screams, with a theatrical hair-pulling gesture, "I knew you'd say that! Gawd, it's getting like script rehearsal—"

She goes on to satirize conversation between us that exaggerates a difficulty she has choosing the right shade of lipstick in the morning and how its significance might lie in a window box of red geraniums that grew outside her mother's bedroom.

"Oh, shit, Judy, I'm sorry," she concludes. "I'm just kind of tired of it all. Truly, I really have learned a lot about myself in here, but I don't *know* why I should want to stop now, and quite frankly, I don't particularly care. Do you have any ideas?"

I put down my coffee and say, "Well, in terms of what's been happening over the last few sessions, I think that what you said before sounds pretty valid to me."

Nancy looks bewildered. "What the hell did I say before?" she questions.

"You suggested that you felt you were getting too dependent on me," I remind her.

"Oh, that. Right. Well, it's true, isn't it?"

"If you feel it, it must be."

"Damn it! Don't do that to me," she protests. "My head's doing somersaults! Don't *you* think I'm too dependent on you? Don't *you* think it would be a good idea for me to be more independent?"

"Absolutely," I concur. "I'm just not sure the most effective way to become more independent is to run away from the problem."

"Why not?" she asks hostilely.

"Because more often than not, you run into somebody else to be dependent on."

She kicks the tip of her patent shoe into a stain on the rug. "So how else do you get over it?" she asks under her breath.

"You tell me."

Nancy makes a little-girl face and says in a sarcastic, nasal singsong, "You stay and work it through."

Then she massages the back of her neck with her hand, closes her eyes, and sighs loudly. We sit in silence a few moments, and she finally drops her hands in her lap and looks at me.

"Look," she says, "let me try it my way. I really want to be on my own for a while. If I get into trouble I'll call you. Okay?"

I point out quietly, "If you want to do it your way, then you don't have to ask my permission, do you?"

"Right on!" she answers angrily. She throws her handbag on the chair, stands up, pulls on her fur coat, then fumbles around with her gloves and turns her head away to hide her tears.

"I suppose I *can* call you if I need you," she says thickly.

"Of course," I answer.

"Take care," Nancy manages in a choked voice. "I'll be

in touch." Significantly perhaps, she leaves the door open as she rushes out.

Already feeling her loss, I make some notes of questions to bring up in supervision about the handling of this separation, her prognosis, and the possibilities of her return to therapy. My own sense is that she may have to run up against her problems of dependency and transference many more times before she decides to try to overcome her fear and really look at them. The last note I make for my supervisor is also for Mel Bernstein. What about the way *I* feel about her leaving?

Elaine fails to keep her appointment on Wednesday. She calls me long-distance during the hour and says she has no money and that her brother-in-law can't drive her to New York till the following week. She turns down the offer of another appointment on the excuse that she doesn't know exactly what day she'll be back and doesn't want me to have to wait again.

"I'll call you when I get there. I can make an appointment then. Except for one thing I can't talk about now, I'm better, so don't worry about me," she says in a strange high-pitched voice I haven't heard before, as though she were disguising the content of her conversation to allay the suspicions of anyone who might be listening.

Closing the office door behind me, I cannot pinpoint the source of my discomfort. It is more than the disappointment of Elaine's not showing. Something about the phone call was subtly but wildly inappropriate.

Dr. White breaks into my thoughts.

"Hello there, stranger! Haven't seen you for weeks. Whatever happened to your catatonic?"

"Oh," I answer absently, "she went home. She decided to come see me as an outpatient, and so far, she's doing okay."

"She doing anything else?" he asks.

"Nope. I'm trying to work toward a day center with her, but so far she hasn't agreed to anything else. But she hasn't relapsed either," I add.

He looks at me over the top of his glasses.

"Don't worry, she will!" he says cheerily. "She will."

At home, a letter from John proposes that I spend a week or two with him in London and the west of Ireland sometime shortly after Easter. A glance outside at the sleet that started around five makes me feel even worse than I've been feeling since Elaine's call. After Easter is over six weeks away. What about the loneliness I'm feeling now?

I think of several people I might call to spend the evening with and come up with a total blank. All the women I feel close to seem to have commitments on Wednesday evenings. There are men who might be available, but none I can think of who mightn't interpret my need for companionship as some sort of sexual overture. Nobody would want to come out on a night like this anyway, and a week night to boot. It occurs to me with a certain humor that it might be an opportune time to invite my editor over to talk about loneliness in shrinks.

Only half serious, I give it up and draw myself a hot bath, remembering John in the bubbles. While the water's running, I find a book and make myself a hot Irish whisky with sugar, lemon, cloves, and boiling water.

Settling into the bath eases some of the neediness, the feeling of wanting to be held and comforted. There are times I have felt overwhelmingly needy. Probably the worst was the period just after Ben and I separated. It occurred to me during that time that I would always be needy, to a greater or lesser degree, and that more likely than not, those needs would never be fully met by other people. There was some real comfort in accepting that as a given about myself, and in realizing that it was probably true for other people as well. There is a space of loneliness that will not be filled, regardless of the turns of time and circumstance. I remember thinking that the realization was not new, that thinkers had written and talked about it, but it had a different impact to discover it for myself and relate it to my day-to-day life.

It rather markedly changed the way I was conducting my behavior at the time. For a while, I had thought about screwing almost anyone available, and for reasons that no doubt had to do with their own hangups, it was clear that almost anyone *was* available. If anything, the de-personalization that resulted in my head from the lack of discrimination made the loneliness even worse.

A friend of mine, June Stein, had been undergoing a similar kind of struggle then. She, in fact, had acted out what I had only been playing with in my head. After working her way through nearly an entire police precinct, she had met me one day and said, "Shit. This is ridiculous. If I'm gonna mess around like this and still be miserable, I might just as well get paid for it."

So June, who has a Ph.D. in French literature, went home and got herself ready. She bathed and brushed her magnificent Russian wolfhound, put on the sexiest dress she could find, quite literally let her hair down (she usually wore it up in a neat bun), took the dog and went strolling provocatively "but tastefully," as she put it, along Central Park South in the early evening. She phoned the next day with her results.

"It was a complete disaster, Judy! Within an hour, no less than seven men tried to pick me up; all well dressed, well groomed, all coming out of places like the Plaza and the St. Moritz, some with chauffeur-driven cars. Oh goody, I thought, it's working! But all that happened was that I got more and more depressed. Everything was fine until they opened their mouths. They were all such schmucks, I just couldn't go through with it! And pretentious schmucks, at that! Give me a nice, clumpy policeman anyday! So anyway, nothing happened. I finally let the last guy pick me up. He seemed kind of sweet, really, and we had a drink together at Trader Vic's."

"So what happened with him?"

"Ech, I just couldn't do it. I was so down by then, I just wanted to go home and knock myself out for the night. Anyway, I don't know how I would have been able to work things out with him."

"Why?"

"He didn't speak a word of English! He was Italian! That's probably why I thought he was so sweet. I couldn't understand a word he said! I give up! Think I'll get into vibrators for a change. Do you know the best kind to buy?"

June eventually decided the problem must be cultural and found herself a job in Paris. She's a lousy correspondent, so I only hope that she found something or someone there to ease the anguish. I had one hurried postcard from her the week of her arrival that reflected some frantic, funny efforts to find an apartment. And nothing since. Not even an address to write to. I hope it's not an indication of where she's at.

The bath and the Irish whisky have lulled me into a comfortable languor. My thoughts turn to John and all the unlikely places we have managed to make love. The day in the Caribbean we had taken off our suits, thinking ourselves safe in the almost deserted spot and atypically opaque sea, which was still sandy and turbulent from a storm the night before. Close to climax, we had been suddenly invaded by a platoon from a Dutch navy vessel which had docked in the island's major harbor that morning. The convoy trucks had lowered their ramps and about 150 men shouting to one another in their native tongue raced into the water around us, splashing, starting spontaneous water fights, laughing, and joking. They took little notice of us.

We were only two heads in the water. Or perhaps they were being polite. At any rate, still intact, we looked at each other and made a silent pact to continue our lovemaking undaunted. With a minimum of movement and expressionless faces, we managed to come in the middle of the Dutch navy. Somehow, we got back into the suits in our hands and swam back to shore.

Later, as we lay basking in the sun on a blanket, a soft-spoken young seaman came over to invite us to join their picnic mess. They had huge caldrons of rather expertly prepared Indonesian food and tubs full of iced beer. We and the other two couples they had invited from the beach got into line in our bathing suits and held our paper plates out to the servers. Several of the men spoke English. They were lovely and charming and gentle, and it was one of the pleasantest meals I can remember. When they had cleaned up and driven away, I wondered about the absurdity of armed men in war in contrast to the peace we had just shared.

The rich, erotic memory stirs my senses, and I leave the bath temporarily to hunt through the refrigerator for a suitably designed vegetable. Though bathwater and a cucumber hardly reduplicate the experience of John and the Caribbean, I am able to have a nice time anyway and achieve an orgasm pretty quickly. Then I get out of the bath feeling relaxed and a little sleepy, make myself another hot whisky, wash and return the cucumber, and fall into a deep, undisturbed sleep.

Early April is hardly an improvement on March, except that the freezing rain and sleet give way to a damp, relentless, bone-chilling drizzle. I gulp down my morning coffee and curse New York under my breath for the dirty tricks it plays on spring and autumn. I climb into some winter clothes that I'm sick and tired of wearing, collect my briefcase, throw on a crumpled raincoat, and decide to walk to work in an effort to defeat my sense of stagnation.

Out on the street, something indefinable makes me feel odd and uncomfortable, but I dismiss it as a projection of my inner discontent and begin the Spartan trudge to the hospital. After a twenty-minute walk, I round a corner and nearly stumble over a pigeon on the sidewalk. The bird scurries out of my path, and something about it, perhaps the fact that it walked rather than flew when I startled it, makes me stop and look more closely. The pigeon has hopped into the gutter and walks along in the muck parallel to the sidewalk ahead of me. Its feathers are patchy and ruffled, and one wing drags lower than the other. It pauses in front of a puddle, jumps back up on the curb, and starts to walk in my direction. For the first time, I notice that the bird is walking at a strange, limping tilt to the ground and has an ugly growth mushrooming out from its underbelly. It cocks its dirty gray head at me. The one red eye that faces me is clouded with a dull, membranous film. I stifle a wave of nausea and walk quickly past it down the street, putting myself down for overdramatizing the episode.

At the hospital, the bird is forgotten in a heavily scheduled morning of conferences and patients. On my way to group supervision with Dr. Gerstein, somebody moves in a dark alcove near the airshaft, and I turn in an instinctive movement of self-protection. A figure crouches on its haunches under the window, shivering. Elaine looks up and recognizes me at the same time.

"Oh, Lord," I say under my breath and put my hand on the thin shoulder under the torn woolen jacket.

"Elaine, where the hell have you been?" I ask gently.

"Judy, I—" She pauses, looks past her apprehensively, and says, "You didn't see a man in the street with red hair and a gray overcoat today, did you?"

"No. Elaine—"

She cuts me off abruptly and continues, "He followed me

here all the way from Wilmington. Treek says he's out to get us. I haven't seen him this morning, but I know he's around somewhere. . . ."

She continues to chronicle the events of the past few weeks in terms of what sounds like a fixed, paranoid delusion. Elaine had previously been overtly paranoid on and off during the course of treatment, but before she had spoken in terms of vague feelings of threat, never focusing on one specific real or imagined group or individual. I glance at my watch and realize that I'm nearly late for supervision. If I don't leave now, it will be the third week in a row that I've failed to be on time, and I'd determined that I wouldn't let it happen again. Dr. Gerstein had jokingly begun to psychoanalyze my tardiness in front of the others, but the humor was wearing thin. Hurriedly, I offer to escort Elaine to the emergency room for a possible admission to the hospital.

"No!" she says defiantly. "I'm not going in there again. There's no need. As long as that man leaves me alone, I'll be okay. Do you have any time to see me today? I have a lot of important things to tell you. God, what's that?"

She starts as a security guard ambles down the hall. Seemingly reassured by his presence, Elaine settles back onto her heels. She looks wasted and filthy, but no worse than a number of other bad times we've shared in the course of our acquaintance. I look through my schedule and give her an appointment for three thirty in exchange for a halfhearted promise that she'll go by herself to the emergency room if she feels more frightened or anxious.

As I walk past Gwen's desk and down the staircase to the other building, Elaine calls after me, "Judy, do you believe about the man?"

"We'll talk about him later," I say over my shoulder as the door swings shut behind me.

I cannot be sure if I hear a despairing, "You don't believe me," as I run to supervision.

As irony would have it, Dr. Gerstein is the late one today. The other residents lounge in his office, discussing post-training plans. Joel Kent fills me in on what's been said.

"What are you gonna do, Judy?" Irene Malin asks me. "Looks like everybody here's going into private practice plus maybe analytic school, except Bob, who wants to earn a lot of money in a Medicaid clinic."

Ignoring her question for the moment, I turn to Bob with surprise for confirmation. "Really, Bob? What are you planning to do?"

He blows his nose and says through a heavy cold, "Irene's right. I'm gonna do general work in a Medicaid clinic for a year at least. You know I finished a residency in medicine before I did psychiatry, right?"

I nod, still confused.

"Well, don't look so surprised," he goes on. "I'm just tired of being poor, that's all. And a wife and kids are expensive. I still owe the government $14,000 for the loans that put me through medical school, just to give you an idea of the kind of debt I'm in. I can always come back to psychiatry."

I interrupt and ask, "But certainly you can earn a better income with a private practice in psychiatry, can't you?"

He laughs and asks me if I was born yesterday.

"Judy, dear, let me open your eyes. I have a friend, Joe Levin, who works in a Medicaid clinic in the Bronx. Guess what he makes practicing medicine there?"

I shrug my shoulders, feeling a little intimidated.

"Between four and five hundred dollars a *day*, depending on the number of patients he sees. Any other questions?" Bob pulls out his handkerchief again and adds through his stuffy nose, "Two years from now, I'll set up a psychiatric office. I want a piece of that pie while it's still there for the taking."

Irene repeats her question while I sit absorbing Bob's

information. I finally reply with my uncertainty.

"There are a few possibilities, Irene. Difficult as they are, I've enjoyed working with psychotics. So I thought I'd either get a part-time hospital job here or go back to the British Isles to work. I'm licensed to practice there, and I kind of miss the atmosphere. I don't know, I keep putting the decision off and probably will continue to until the last minute. I keep hoping it will be made for me somehow. The only thing I know for certain is that wherever I am, I'd like to devote part of my time to working with psychotic patients."

Joel mutters good-naturedly around his pipe. "What are you, crazy or something?"

"Don't be so casual, Joel," I laugh. "I've often questioned my motivations, and that's one of the possible explanations."

He grins and says, "Takes one to know one, huh?"

I nod agreeably.

Irene talks about studying further in child psychiatry, and Joel mentions that he has been reading and comparing the literature from the various institutes for advanced analytic training. We rap for another thirty minutes, and the others get up to leave.

Bob looks at his watch and says, "In college and med school, we'd give the professors twenty minutes. A half hour's too long to wait for anyone."

Since I made such a point of getting there, I decide to wait another five or ten minutes. I start to browse through the books on the shelves when Dr. Faulkner walks by, sees me, and comes in.

"Whatcha doin'?"

"Hi. Waiting for Dr. Gerstein for supervision."

He drops into a chair and says, "Nat's not coming in this afternoon. Didn't he leave word for you?"

"Not that I know of, but the new department secretary's out to lunch, and she may have forgotten to leave us a note," I respond, replacing a book by Searles.

He asks for a follow-up on Beth, and I bring him up to date on our sessions. He listens chin in hand and finally comments, "So! You've 'cured' her, have you?"

I shake my head and tell him about Dr. White's predictions, admitting to fears that one day they may turn out to be true.

"Despite all the 'insights' she's achieved, Dr. Faulkner, she doesn't budge an inch from that hotel except to have meals with her mother or come for her appointment with me. She's resisted every effort I've made to get her into a day program."

He argues, "But she seems to have held her own for a couple of months now. What's your concern?"

I tell him of my planned vacation during Easter and Beth's refusal to see any other therapist in my absence.

"Without any other support system," I speculate, "I think she may just slip back again, with a little help from her mother, while I'm away. It's been a tedious, uphill battle; I'd hate to come back and find all our work destroyed."

Dr. Faulkner muses with his hands behind his head. He glances absently at the returning secretary, who pauses in taking off her coat to answer the phone.

"Well," he says with a half-smile, "it's that old psychotic bargain again."

"What's that?" I ask, already suspecting the answer.

"Adopt me completely or else!" he laughs.

"I'm afraid so," I say dispiritedly.

Dr. Faulkner leans over and pats my hand. "Well, Judy, don't count on it. Patients have a habit of surprising one sometimes. You may come back and find her even better than when you left. You may even—"

He stops abruptly and looks inquisitively at the door. I turn to see the new secretary standing there with a look of horror on her face.

"Are you Dr. Benetar?" she asks.

I nod with a sense of foreboding.

"This phone call is for you. I think the man on the other end said that one of your patients jumped out a window of the outpatient department building."

I get up mechanically, go to the phone, and listen to the voice of a detective who sounds as though he's seen just about everything give an accurate description of Elaine. Monotonously, he lists the familiar contents of her shopping bag, found next to her under the eighth-floor window from which she jumped, while I keep hoping to wake up from the nightmare.

The voice goes on laconically, "I'm afraid you'll have to come over and identify the body, doctor. We can't seem to locate any of the relatives. We'll meet you by the secretary's desk here on the eighth floor."

"Judy, stop," Dr. Faulkner calls after me. "You've forgotten your handbag, briefcase, and coat. Here, let me help you on with it."

He guides my arms into the sleeves and grasps my shoulders for a minute.

"Sons of bitches," he says, "I'm sure they don't really need your identification. Why don't you stay here and I'll go and get you a stiff drink."

The secretary stands absolutely motionless, ossified.

Without bothering to reply, I start to walk out of the room, shocked and numb with a sense of reality-unreality. Dr. Faulkner asks if I want him to go with me and I shake my head and leave.

Gwen is completely hysterical when I arrive on the floor. Some of the workers from the community psychiatry department are making attempts to calm her.

When she sees me, she cries through mascara-smudged eyes, "Judy, I couldn't help it! I couldn't help it! I saw her open the window and I ran to get the security guard. When we got back, she was already gone. I couldn't help it! I never could have stopped her by myself, I'm too little! I couldn't help it!"

Somehow, through the haze, I manage to say something mechanically reassuring. A pale, heavy-set man in plain clothes asks me to accompany him to the street level for the identification. The word seems to have spread quickly. Two of my friends from day center get off the elevator and walk with me for support, silent and shaky themselves, no doubt reliving Joanna's plunge from the same building a few months before.

A policeman has been posted at the site. My friends stop a few hundred yards away and say they'll wait.

"Sorry, Judy, we just can't face it. We'll wait here for you." And then, under her breath, I hear Rita say, "Jesus, I'm glad I'm not a doctor."

Stupidly puzzling over the remark, I find my legs walking beside the detective up to a somber-looking patrolman and a figure covered by an army blanket.

"All right, officer," the detective says, and I stifle an impulse to stop the policeman from lifting the blanket.

Elaine has landed face-down, and there is none of the grotesque disfiguration I had dreaded. She lies almost in the position of a sleeping child, with one hand up near her mouth. The exposed side of her face is unmarred and the eye is closed. The cement has been cracked and broken in places by the assaults of many long winters. The slab under Elaine's head slants slightly downward away from her body. It carries a dark stream of blood from somewhere beneath her face to a small pool about a foot away. Fighting a growing cloudiness, I gradually become aware of the detective's colorless voice repeating the same question for a second time.

"I beg your pardon?"

With the faintest hint of annoyance, he reiterates patiently, "I said, can you identify this woman as your patient, Elaine Carson?"

"Yes."

"Are you absolutely certain?" he says tiredly, as though he has been through this routine a hundred times before.

"Yes."

"You can't see much of her face from here. Are you sure?" he persists. "Did you see her in those clothes today?"

"Yes."

"What time?" he asks.

"About an hour ago, I think."

"Did she give you any indication that she was upset?"

"She was always upset."

"Did she give you any indication that she intended to commit suicide?"

I find myself vaguely irritated by the seeming stupidity of his question, but cannot find the energy to be angry.

"No."

The patrolman shocks me out of my stupor.

"Do you want me to turn her over, sergeant?"

"No!" I shout. "Don't, please!"

The detective seems to remember that not everyone lives his kind of life and becomes a little more human.

"Hang on there, doctor. You're doing fine." He turns to the policeman and says, "No, that's okay, Gus. You can cover her up again."

He leads me back to his car and pulls out a clipboard, where he records bits of information I give him about Elaine. Then he thanks me and returns to the building. I turn down the offer of companionship from my anxious friends, and they return to their work. I stand on the corner, trying to think what to do next and struggling dully to remember my schedule for the rest of the afternoon. I realize that I have to cancel two appointments with the secretary. Numbly crossing the street, I make my way back to the main office and find Dr. Faulkner waiting there.

"You all right?" he says.

When I nod, he asks if I'd like to have that drink now.

"No thanks. If you don't mind, I think I'd rather just go home."

"Sure," he replies.

When I start to give instructions to the secretary, Dr. Faulkner tells me my schedule's been taken care of already. I thank him and leave.

Outside on the street, I meet Dr. Dunbar, who reminds me that he wants me to talk to some medical students interested in psychiatry next Tuesday.

"By the way," he says as an afterthought, "I heard about your patient. Too bad. It happens to all of us, you know. But cheer up, the first one's always the worst."

I suppress an urge to say something obscene in response to his remark and passively let him help me into a taxi.

It is late when the cats wake me, crying to be fed. Feeling confused and disoriented, I get up and switch on the light, trying vainly to remember how I happened to be on the floor rather than the bed. I look at my watch. Past eight o'clock. In the middle of opening a can of cat food, the full horror of the day's events sweeps over me with a tangible force. I barely make it to the sink in time to vomit into it. The physical activity somehow triggers the emotions I have managed to repress to this moment, and I stand there over the drain, retching and sobbing and choking. Clyde rubs himself against my elbow, then climbs up onto my shoulder, purring absurdly into my ear. I shake him off and turn on the faucet, leaning my forehead against the spigot, dry-heaving and gasping for breath. The phone rings about five times and stops, then rings again and finally gives up. The loud distraction diverts my attention enough to allow me to spoon the cat food into the bowls. When I put the dishes down, I apologize to Clyde for his rude handling. He ignores me and settles down to his smelly fish. I stand there, staring dumbly at the two cats eating side by side, struck by the absurd continuation of things familiar. How can they be doing what they always do?

Without knowing quite how it happened, I find myself dialing a number by the light that filters in from the other room.

I hear a voice saying, "Hello? Hello, is someone there?" and then remember the person I've called.

"Mel? Mel, it's me, Judy."

"Judy Benetar? Hi—is something wrong? What's the matter? What's happened?"

The concern in his voice enables me to complete a full sentence.

"Elaine jumped out a window today and I had to go identify her."

After a shocked silence, he says simply, "That's a tough one. Hold on, let me go get my appointment book."

He puts the receiver down, and I can hear children laughing in the background while I wait. Sam walks away from his dish, leaving the usual morsel in one corner for later. He sits down nearby and begins to wash his face with a paw.

"Hello, Judy? Can you be here by seven fifteen tomorrow morning?"

"Yes, I think so," I hear myself answer.

"Okay. See you then. Is there anyone there with you now?" he asks.

"No. I don't want anyone."

"What have you been doing?"

"Nothing."

The background noise on his end is growing raucous. He puts his hand over the receiver and says something. When he comes back on, it is quieter, and I hear him ask me if I have any Valium in the house.

"I think I have a sample somewhere," I manage to recall.

"Okay. After you hang up, will you go and take ten milligrams of Valium and a shot of brandy if you have any, and then get into bed?"

"Yes, all right," I answer.

"Good. See you at seven fifteen," he repeats and hangs up.

I find the medication behind some cold cream in the medicine chest, take out two of the scored yellow pills, and wash them down with half a tumbler of cognac. Somehow it is important to be very clean and warm before I fall asleep. From the laundry chest, I take a set of fresh sheets and pillowcases and change all the linen on the bed. On an empty stomach, the liquor hits me quickly, and I am just able to take a quick hot shower and get into a clean flannel nightgown before drifting into a welcome oblivion with the cats curled up at the foot of the bed.

I sleep through the appointment with Mel Bernstein the next morning. At a quarter to eight, I wake up and phone him. The only other appointment he can give me is for five thirty.

"Should I go to work, Mel?" I ask, feeling slightly light-headed and annoyed that I have overslept.

"Depends on what would make you feel realer," he says, before he hangs up.

It's a toss-up, but the prospect of spending the day in an empty apartment seems slightly worse than having to make it through a day at the hospital, so I force myself to get dressed and make some coffee and toast.

Ironically, the weather has cleared, and rays of morning light come streaming through the kitchen window, somehow making me feel even more oppressed. The good-humored newscaster says it will be a day of seasonable temperatures for the first time this spring.

"It's out of keeping," I say flatly. Sam looks up and responds in Siamese. Clyde looks at me sleepily from a patch of sun.

I take another Valium before leaving the apartment.

The day is an odd composite of the impressions of two inner people. One of them sees patients, talks to fellow residents and supervisors, signs requisitions, and answers phone messages as though nothing had happened. The other stands apart in dumb horror and disbelief, frantically trying to will an undoing.

There are supportive remarks by a few experienced colleagues. Well-intentioned, helpful comments that hardly make a dent in my growing sense of guilt:

"Rough—I know how you feel."

"The only way is to let time pass, let your head work it through, go over it and over it and over it, talk it with people you trust, eat it, drink it, sleep it and dream it, and gradually it won't hurt quite so much."

"You know that the experts who have success with people like Elaine also have a long-term structure to back up the work they do; places like Austin-Riggs and Chestnut Lodge where the patients can live comfortably and freely in an ideal treatment setting; all they need is to be young, intelligent, schizophrenic, and have forty thousand dollars a year to pay for their keep."

"Face it. If you're going to take on people like her, you also have to be prepared to take on the risks that come with them. . . . Did you ever stop to think about the odds against a twenty-five-year-old woman with multiple hospitalizations and three or four previous suicide attempts . . . just unfortunate that the successful attempt happened to be at your expense. . . ."

Larry and Alan take me and Lois Birnbaum out for a Chinese meal, tactfully making no attempts to draw me into their talk. They order a sea bass smothered in hot garlic sauce on a bed of soft noodles, several rounds of cocktails, and four cold beers to go with the food. In gentle defiance of the oppressiveness of the atmosphere, they carry on a ribald conversation vaguely reminiscent of a Marx Brothers' routine. The meal lasts for over three hours, at the end of which I gratefully realize that the working day is nearly over.

I return to the residents' lounge and, not trusting my state of mind, make a list of things I have to do in the coming week. Glancing over it, it looks insurmountable. Dr. Dunbar goes by and reminds me again about the conference with the medical students. Stan calls and asks for an extra appointment. Beth's mother has left a message that she would like to meet with me and discuss a plan for her daughter. The secretary starts to question me about another matter. The clock says five to five, and something in my head clicks "no more." I pick up my coat and walk out.

In the cab on the way to Mel Bernstein's, I tell myself that I will not let anything touch me again. No more pain. No more demands. No more guilt. No more attempts to find answers. No more playing God.

In Mel's waiting room, I think about careers in marine biology and oceanography. The patient ahead of me leaves, and Mel ushers me into his office. We sit down, he looks at me, and I burst into tears. He hands me a box of tissues and makes no attempt to interfere.

Finally, I am able to tell him the story, to which he listens without interruption. When I stop talking, he says, "Why would she want to do such an angry thing to you?"

"I don't know!" I wail. "I guess I didn't help her enough. I feel like I must have missed something or that I did something wrong. I guess I didn't realize how much trouble she was in."

He responds with a seeming non sequitur. "Besides guilt, can you sort out any of the other things you're feeling?"

It takes me several minutes to reply.

"Loss. She was like a relative to me in some ways. She was the first long-term patient I took on, and I worked so hard with her; she became a significant part of my life. I'm really going to miss her as a person, Mel."

He nods and waits while I weep my way through a few more tissues.

Then I stare at the wall of books and say, "Anger. I feel so cheated, so let down. It just pisses me off so, that she didn't give us more of a chance. We'd really made some strides toward a sense of separateness, a sense of independence for her."

"Yes, I think you had," Mel says, "but you realize that as schizophrenics become more autonomous, their potential for suicide increases."

"Thanks. Now you tell me," I snap at him.

He passes the waste basket to me for the lapful of soiled tissues, and says, "Anything else you feel?"

"No. That's all."

"Are you sure?"

I search my soul and start to shake my head, when it occurs to me with a thud that I also feel a strong sense of relief.

"Why does that surprise you?" Mel asks.

"But it's terrible, Mel! How can I be relieved that Elaine's dead?"

He asks *me* to tell *him*.

"I guess I'm relieved that she doesn't have to suffer anymore. Almost every minute of her life was a kind of torment, a deadly struggle to be free of pain and fear. She lost, but at least it's ended."

I think it over for a minute and then add, "And I guess I'm relieved for myself that I don't have to watch it anymore or worry about trying to do something about it. But that makes me feel guilty again, and the whole cycle starts all over. Well, no more. This is it."

Mel interrupts when I start to tell him my thoughts about leaving psychiatry. He says with a hint of anger, "What makes you think you're so special?"

I look up in surprise.

He goes on, "Who do you think you are that you

shouldn't have to cope with failures and disappointments like the rest of us lowly mortals, the Queen of Sheba? And what do you think you're doing, subjugating your talent and ability to a wounded vanity? Do you think you're the first psychiatrist ever to lose a patient? Is *your* pain so poignant, so separate, so different? There's a lot you can learn from this experience, if you can get beyond your own tarnished pride and start to look at it."

After a moment of embarrassment in the face of his uncharacteristic outburst, I manage to say, "Thanks. I guess I deserved that."

During the exchange that follows for the remainder of the hour, I have the peculiar sensation of being in touch with something that I value, and it doesn't dawn on me until just before I leave that what I value is the experience of being alive itself, and that, despite my loss, the awful events of the day before have in no way diminished that sense of appreciation. Mel intuitively stops talking and watches my face.

He raises his eyebrows questioningly and I say, "You know, Mel, I'm really very tough."

He laughs and responds, "Is that why your hands are shaking and your lips trembling? But I think I know what you mean."

Outside, the blue of early evening has settled over the city. The air has a promise of warmth. It carries a scent of wet earth from the park, which tempts me to take a long walk. I stop somewhere on the way at a brightly lit delicatessen, and sometime well after dark I arrive home and unwrap a package of smoked Irish salmon to share with a couple of hungry cats.